FULLY ALIVE

Awakening Health, Humor, Compassion and Truth

3RD EDITION

FULLY ALIVE

Awakening Health, Humor, Compassion and Truth

3rd Edition

Foreword by Lynn V. Andrews

LOUISE LEBRUN

MANJUL
Manjul Publishing House Pvt. Ltd.

Published in India by

MANJUL

Manjul Publishing House Pvt. Ltd.

10, Nishat Colony, Bhopal, INDIA - 462003

Phone : +91-755-4240340, Fax : +91-755-2736919

E-mail : manjul@manjulindia.com

Website : www.manjulindia.com

First published - 2008

ISBN 978 - 81 - 8322 - 106 - 1

Cover Design by: Karina Evangelista, Montreal, Quebec, Canada

Printed & bound in India by

Thomson Press (India) Ltd.

Dedication

To those awakened and awakening souls
whose curiosity is greater than their need to be right; and
whose courage is the context within which their fear unfolds.

Table of Contents

Table of Contents

List of Figures

Acknowledgments

I am deeply grateful to the many people who have contributed to the development of this work, either by direct intention or osmosis.

First, my special thanks to Lynn Andrews for the profound and lasting impact of her evolution on my own. Long before it was popular or fashionable, Lynn stood tall in the truth of her own experience, sharing her journey of discovery and offering the opportunities it carried to all who were willing to travel with her . From her, I learned to trust what moved inside me and to rise to the full measure of my own potential. Her work made it possible for me to reconsider and redefine power in a way that has become profoundly meaningful to me. It has influenced who I have become as a woman, as a mother and as a force of manifestation in our world.

My thanks to Wayne Dyer for the lesson of his constant growth as evidenced in his continuously evolving body of work. It is less about what he says and so much more about who he chooses to continue to become. And to Joseph Chilton Pearce, Candace Pert, Bruce Lipton, Paul Goodwin and Deepak Chopra for the miracles that their world-views and their science allow us to invite into our daily lives. Each of them has influenced the way my thinking has evolved. A special thanks to Diane Fassel for being a living example of what compassion under fire actually looks like.

I have been greatly influenced by the courage and persistence of Jane Roberts and Robert Butts in their commitment to share the Seth material with the rest of the world; by J.Z. Knight for her tireless efforts in bringing us the Ramtha material; and by Serge Kahili King for his informative and highly readable works on Huna. Their courage and willingness to take risks has been a living example to me of how to speak my own truth – no matter what!

My deepest gratitude and affection go out to all who are and have been my clients. You have trusted me with your darkest secrets and most fragile moments. Your generosity of spirit and your willingness to open your heart to me have proven over and over again the determination we carry, as human beings, to be whole. You have made it possible for me to learn how to live comfortably, with trust and hope, in the courage of those larger questions.

Foreword
by Lynn V. Andrews

Shamanism in the 21st century is to me a way of understanding and developing one's spiritual enlightenment. When you think that a society grows out of the language that it speaks, and you look at the English-speaking world which is so often a pragmatic and generally materialistic society, you realize that the practice of any religious or sacred art can be a very difficult task

We have very few words in our language to describe evolution into spiritual consciousness and realization. When we use a term like *shamanism,* in a sense it means something different to everyone using it. The word *shaman* comes from the Tungusic language of Siberia, to describe "a priest or priestess who uses magic for the purpose of curing the sick, divining the hidden, and controlling events." (**Merriam Webster's Collegiate Dictionary** [Tenth Ed.]) It has been adopted into the English language to describe a native healer who is usually born into a long line of medicine men or women and/or who is taught the healing arts from birth.

There are also other kinds of shaman healers. One is a person who is simply born with a mark, whatever that mark may be in the native tradition that the person is born to. Another is one who is born into a life situation where she nearly loses her life in some life-defying situation. This person lives through the experience and comes out on the other side with very special abilities. This person is a shaman who heals differently and may not be part of a medicine tradition in any given tribe. These latter shamans are wounded healers. They are extraordinary men and women who have developed the art of Seeing; they can choreograph the energies of the universe in a way that brings healing and light into people's lives.

FOREWORD

Every shaman is different. Every nation of native people is different. Their guardians, their ruling icons are vastly diversified, but the source of power is always the same. There is always the firstness of woman, the understanding that power comes from Mother Earth and Father Sky; there are always the elementals, the directions and the unseen mysteries and powers of the other dimensions of reality.

We all as human beings are looking for the meaning of life. We all experience disease, not only of the physical body but also of the spirit. Shamans help you to balance the physical state with the spiritual, the known with the unknown. I think it is very important in this time of stress, this time of environmental disillusionment, that we understand as a people that no one owns the truth and that each and every one of us, no matter who we are, is an expression of life that is a part of the Great Spirit that animates us. This is a time that we need to reach across racial, societal and religious barriers and join hands with our sisters and brothers to heal this planet and to heal ourselves.

Shamanism is about the end of duality. It is about oneness with all of the energies that surround you. If you do not understand the oneness of energy, you do not understand the laws of power. The first lesson of power is that we are all alone. And then there is a giant abyss between this statement and the last lesson of power, which is that we are all one. The last lesson of power is the oneness of us all, the respect and the honor given to different ideologies and thought, not war between those ideologies, but honor.

People around this earth are looking desperately for the reason for life, the understanding of God in our lives. When someone is trying to find the meaning of life through the practice of ancient ritual, perhaps using drums and sage, is that person not doing what ancient peoples wanted from the beginning? The ancient peoples wanted everyone who discovered them to understand their way of life. People who are hungering to go back to the earth, to understand the shamanic harmonies of life, the magic of life, the understanding that there are physical and spiritual dimensions that can be united in a life of wholeness, are also trying to heal the earth through the process of healing themselves.

To be a shaman is very different from being interested in shamanism. A shaman has a true gift and has been touched by spirit. That person is "one-who-knows-how" in the words of my teachers. She knows how to understand the universe, how to travel in the dimensions of reality and power that most people have neither the desire nor the focus to travel. She is neither more nor less important than those who have no desire to follow this path. She simply is what she is.

The process of shamanism is a process of growth and effort and focus that brings people into balance with the world around them. It is a process of love. I am often stunned when I work with people who have become identified with the technique of their job. Our world, our society seems to reward those who become centered on the idea of more and bigger and more powerful at all costs. Lost in that rush of effort is the artifice, the enjoyment of the process. Lost in that rush is the love for what you do. Shamanism as I have experienced it is the love of life, the profound love for healing and harmony and balance between the physical world and the world of profound joyous spirit. There is no way to explain the face of Great Spirit once you have experienced that face. You can describe how you feel when you see the face; you can describe the stillness at the center of the storm, the flowing bliss that courses through your veins. But you cannot describe the beauty that is expressed except by the love of process and the grace that comes from that.

A shaman is one who has been gifted with spirit, with the knowledge of spirit, the knowing of mystery. And you can witness in that person the years and years of study, of practice, of work to learn and hone these gifts into a laser beam of effective light that can be directed at any given disease to reconstitute a reflection of perfect light and health. A shaman has mastered his technique. A shaman has understood intimately the tools of her trade. But a shaman is not identified with those tools nor with the technique, because a true shaman has a perfect balance between technique and the love of the process and the art of what he or she is accomplishing to promote harmony and balance between all living things. (***Writing Spirit***, by Lynn Andrews. New York NY: Jeremy P. Tarcher/Penguin Books Inc., 2006.)

Throughout her work, author and WEL-Systems® creator Louise LeBrun follows the scientific approach to wellness, and she brings with her an exceptional ability to perceive what is not intended within the syllogisms and formulas of mathematical exploration. Oftentimes I have said that the great worth within a piece of writing is not the words themselves, necessarily, but the power and strength that exists between the words.

When scientists explored the atom, they found that at the center of the atom was a nothingness that couldn't be explained or mathematically divined. The human brain uses only a small percentage of its capabilities in the process of everyday thinking. And yet how does one measure the abstract?

When a shaman moves into his or her power, she moves into a place of heightened perception and awareness. Oftentimes the shaman will move into the universe outside the self, but more likely she brings the universe within herself alive in order to explore a world that is retained within each and every living being on this earth.

Louise understands with unique capability the existence of life force and the special, unknowable world that lives with such vitality all around us. To see a scientist who is able to know that something exists without an explanation is to see a woman who is blazing a whole new trail into our world of extraordinary mystery and challenge. A shaman wanders this mystical path from moment to moment, always measuring, always testing the strength or the fluidity of a matrix of life-giving fibers. A shaman does not explain what she is doing. She simply knows.

I would consider Louise LeBrun a scientist who is within this special realm of knowing, and who with great humor and care and love -- besides all of her science-minded acumen -- is expressing it and sharing it with others in her marvelous books.

Fully Alive: Awakening Health, Humor, Compassion and Truth is a remarkable exploration into our ordinary lives in an extraordinary and transformative way.

Lynn Andrews

Author of 19 books and workbooks on spirituality and personal healing, including the ***New York Times*** *and internationally bestselling "Medicine Woman" series.* ***Medicine Woman****, now in its 48th printing, just celebrated its 25th anniversary with the publication of a special anniversary edition by Tarcher/Penguin Books; her latest book,* ***Writing Spirit****, is now available in paperback.*

Lynn is a 21st century mystic, shaman healer and teacher who has spent the last 40 years of her life studying and working with an ancient society of native women healers, from the far north of Canada to the Yucatán, from Aboriginal Australia to the Tibetan Himalayas. Her ground-breaking work has received international acclaim and she is recognized as one of the world's leading experts on spirituality and personal development. She is the founder of the Lynn Andrews Center for Sacred Arts and Training. You can learn more about Lynn by visiting her website at www.lynnandrews.com.

FULLY ALIVE

Come to the edge, he said
They said, we are afraid
Come to the edge, he said
They came, he pushed them....
And they flew.

-Guillaume Apollinaire-

Preface – Third Edition

It's been almost seven years since first publishing 'Fully Alive from 9 to 5'. I wrote it because I felt it was important for us, as human beings, to have a different framework or context from which to consider our individual selves as well as our collective humanity. Not only am I even more convinced of that today than I was then, it now presents with an even greater sense of urgency.

I am very mindful of the degree to which we continue to seek - outside of ourselves - a teacher/guide/mentor/guru/religion/fix/formula/answer that will result in us feeling better about ourselves and the world that we are creating. Unfortunately, decades of just such a search have proven, at least to me, that it is not going to happen that way. As a friend of mine says: "If white light and forgiveness were going to do, it would have happened by now!" My sentiments, exactly.

From the beginning, *Fully Alive* was intended to offer an alternative to how we see ourselves – not just ***who*** we are as individuals but ***what*** we are as human beings. Written as an invitation and not a command performance, my intention was and still is to offer a ***wake-up*** call to us all, that we might begin to notice that we are the very thing that we seek. It occurred to me one day that in 2500 years, when archeologists are uncovering the remnants of our current civilization and are marveling at the 'wisdom of the ancients', we already are the 'ancients' whose wisdom they will be seeking. It may do us well to begin to pay attention to that *now,* while we can still have an impact on our own lives and the reality that we create, collectively.

PREFACE

The third edition of *Fully Alive* reflects some of my own evolution. Mindful that I've now written other books that offer more beyond what you'll read here (books like *Phoenix Rising: The Freeing of Human Potential*, and *When the Horse Dies, Get Off... and Stop Dragging It Around!*, that did not exist at the time of first publishing), it has become clear to me that I need to be more direct about what is possible for you and for me, through this very different way of seeing ourselves and the world around us.

In this third edition, you'll continue to read about work. However, when you do, begin to consider work beyond the 'fact' of your Monday to Friday experience and also consider it as a metaphor in your life. How you move through your work is a reflection of how you move through your life. Given that we spend more time at work than we do anywhere else as adults, consider the immense opportunity that 'work' offers for us to begin to redirect our attention and notice *ourselves* instead of everyone else. Think of our work environments as a living laboratory for discovering more about how we move through life and how else we might engage. So, although you will continue to read about work/life, begin to think more along the lines of life/work with your reality as the tangible, living reflection of your choices and your results.

You'll notice that there is also a new first chapter that speaks to a more intense and powerful context for you to consider as you read this book. As much as it continues to be an invitation, this one has an edge. It carries with it a sense of urgency; a sense of an unfolding density and intensity of result that (I believe, as do so many others) we can no longer just notice and push out of our awareness. So, be warned: take nice, long, slow deep breaths as you move through Chapter 1. Don't resist or push back and shut down the information that begins to move in your body. Stop when you need to and allow yourself to read and re-read as many times as you would like to. You'll be glad you did. Quantum TLC™ (as explained and described in *Phoenix Rising: The Freeing of Human Potential*) isn't just a technique – it's a powerful way to live. Breathing in... breathing out... and in the process of doing just that, discovering more of who and what you are.

You'll also find a significant chunk of new information that has been added to this edition. The chapter on 'Claiming It' now includes information that addresses the impact of our family of origin on how we get to be who we are; how we move through the world and make choices and create; and how we determine, at a very early age, what works and what doesn't work in staying safe and managing in our world. Family systems roles (like Family Hero, Lost Child, Scapegoat and Mascot) may cause you to feel many different things – from a sense of deep relief to intense discomfort to a sense of freedom and new beginnings. No matter what you experience, remember to breathe and stay focused on what you want.

Which begs the question: what do you want? Why are you reading this book? What are you looking for? All of these questions presuppose that you don't already have what you're looking for; that you're not already who you want to become. My intention is that by the end of reading this book, you'll feel very differently about that. That's the good news! Here's the bad news: once you know that, there is no one but *you* to turn to. Nothing outside of you – no guru, no dogma, no fix/answer, etc – will ever be able to take the glory or the blame for the life you're creating. It's all yours – to do with as you see fit. And whatever you've got, rest firmly in knowing that it is your own creation.

Perhaps a new question becomes: are you willing to own your own creations? Like we cannot see our own faces and must rely on reflection in order for us to 'know', so our lives are the reflection of the structures of who we are. Once you know that, who else can you possibly point to as being responsible for your life?

Long ago, Wayne Dyer wrote: "We are not human beings having a spiritual experience, but spiritual beings having a human experience". I don't doubt that for a moment and yet, we seem to insist on standing in our humanity to look out and over at our spirituality in order to explore it. It leaves us wishing and wanting and hoping and not necessarily very different in how we move through the world.

Imagine how our lives – and our world! – might unfold were we to choose to stand in our spirituality and look out and over at our humanity. What might we discover about that flesh-and-bone expression of the godforce that we already are? How else might we consider creating our Selves, our lives and our world? From that place, there is nothing that can stop us from being the magnificent Creation-Force that each of us is!

Louise LeBrun

June 2007

Introduction

My journey has been a long one. Along the way, there have been many challenges, not the least of which were multiple 'addictions' including alcohol abuse, eating disorders and work obsession, and a nervous breakdown. There were times when I doubted that I would make it and others when I wasn't sure I wanted to. Yet it has all brought me to who I have become today. This book is my act of courage. It will stand forever as a reminder to me of the power of trusting myself; of moving away from what's 'right' and moving into what's right for me.

Like many of you, I was well-educated, well-read and well-informed. I said the right things and spent time with the right people. I was nobody's fool: intelligent, articulate, quick-witted, determined, committed and hard-driving, I was a paragon of the virtue that was the feminist era. My bedside companions were the Harvard Business Review, the Economist and Fortune Magazine. Not a day/week/month went by that I did not voraciously read, from cover to cover, the advice offered and then seek out with a vengeance the books and articles referenced, for further development.

And yet even with all that information - all that analysis, logic and rigorous intellectual pursuit; all those facts and case studies and *how-to's* - about work and life, mine fell apart. Like Humpty Dumpty, putting the pieces back together again became not only an impossible task but one which I desperately avoided by continuing to be ill for close to five months. As long as I stayed sick, I did not have to return to my barren, rigid and lifeless existence. I did not like who I had become.

All along the path of my own development, I sought to find the answers: from parents, teachers, bosses, books, audio products, courses, coaches, therapists, systems, etc. And all along that path, the recommended answers proved to be a betrayal of *my own* truth, *my own* creativity and *my own* intuitive awareness. As I persisted in embracing what others thought I should, my body screamed its objections and flaunted its defiance. It almost cost me my life.

Someone once said: "If you want to change your life, you must first change the way that you perceive life". Little did I know how unprepared I was for just such a shift in perception, even a very small one. With a small shift in perception comes tremendous power and leverage - to change your thoughts, to change your life and to change the world in which you live. Think of the discovery and the power that came with a shift in perception from a flat world to one that is round; from the certainty of Newtonian physics to a quantum world. A shift in perception from an allopathic perspective to a quantum biological one may well mean the difference between a cycle of life in decline and the creation of one that thrives.

Change perception and everything else changes all by itself

Change perception and everything else changes all by itself: the things we are willing to do and those we are not willing to do; the places we go; the people we spend time with; the words that come out of our mouths; the systems we support; the very world in which we live and call, with such great certainty, "reality". There was a time when the idea that the world was flat was not an opinion, it was 'fact' and 'true' and 'real'. We now know that the idea that the world was flat was a perception. Until that perception changed, people did not venture forth. Once that perception changed, the world expanded: ships sailed, commerce exploded, cultures migrated. The world was no longer the same or ever capable of being the same again, given what we now perceived and 'knew'. And all of this was preceded by a simple shift in perspective which created the context within which the new order unfolded.

Not only the choices we made but our very *capacity for choosing*, exploded. In the blink of an eye, reality as we had defined it ceased to exist and was replaced by a far more vast potential - the possibility of more and greater and further, to move into what we were capable of becoming.

Power resides in the capacity to choose, not in the choice itself. We have grown up in cultures where we are ill-prepared to even know the meaning of choosing. Rarely do we know how to distinguish between an option and an authentic choice - one of our own creation. We are well trained to follow the rules: to consult with authority, to defer to the collective view. We are not encouraged to challenge the status quo but to embrace it; to run with the pack rather than to travel alone. Homogeneity and group-think are the expectation. Survival is in the collective, in that group-think and that group-speak. This perspective is destined to limit human expression since the process of embracing the status quo leads to eating your own tail. Eventually, you disappear.

Power resides in the capacity to choose, not in the choice itself

And we are disappearing. Our capacity for joy, for play, for delighting in our own existence is rapidly disappearing. We have become slaves to our own rules. Once again, we live in a time when the masses are controlled by a handful - whether in work systems, community systems, religious systems or your own home. The very thought of having to think for ourselves, without the benefit of precedent to follow or handbook to consult, causes beads of sweat to form on our brow and our stomachs to burn and churn. We have become dependent on antacids and antidepressants to get us through our days - and worse, our nights. We have lost our nerve for trusting our own intelligence, our own wisdom. We no longer trust our ability to navigate by the stars of our own inner truth. No case study will ever give that back to you. Rigorous analysis will not give you back your nerve. That is something you must take back - by instinct, and alone.

Like you, I was trained to believe - without question - that work was no place for the personal. Work was professional and feelings were personal. At the very least, bringing my feelings to work was 'unprofessional' or worse, a symbol of my total ineptitude and lack of discipline. Objectivity and emotions were mutually exclusive. And yet today science tells us that objectivity is an illusion; that the observer affects the observed. That indeed, the observer is a part of the very formulation of what we experience as the product.

For decades, we have fooled ourselves into believing that work is public and that our feelings are private; that work is objective and our feelings are subjective, and never the two should meet. For decades we have lied to ourselves and each other in the hopes of preserving what we have all known, deep inside ourselves, to be that lie. To know the lie is one thing; to live it, day after day after day, will kill you. If not in body, then in spirit and in your desire to go on.

To know the lie is one thing; to live it, day after day after day, will kill you

Seeking to be whole

This book brings these two things together. It integrates the personal and the professional, the private and the public you. It challenges the illusion that work is public, professional and impersonal. Work is nothing but personal, given that the only thing going on at work *is* people - like you and me - interacting with each other. And people are very personal. The perception that work is public and professional prevents us from achieving what we are looking for. First, our perception must change then the rest will follow.

For far too long, we've defined the problems of work as work problems. It's not about work – it's about us. If we were to raise our thinking to a higher level, we might notice that work is a by-product of who we are; a symptom of a process that we have created first from 'being' then from 'doing'. The 'problem' lies in the fact that we have forgotten that it is our own creation. We can't change work. We can however, change ourselves and given that we spend more time at work than anywhere else in our lives, when we change who we are at work that change will significantly affect the quality of our lives at all levels.

Our solution to any problem is dependent on the way that we define the problem; the way we put shape to it and name it. As long as we focus our attention on 'work' (which we think is 'out there'), we give ourselves permission to not pay attention to ourselves (which we know is 'in here'). For very good reasons which we'll cover in later chapters, we would much prefer to tolerate and distract ourselves with the discomforts of work than wander into the unknown landscapes of what lives inside us. We've been taught to believe that danger lurks in its darkened corners and bottomless holes. We've perfected our strategies for staying clear of the body's efforts to get our attention. And yet, what also lingers there is the vast, untouched pool of our own potential, just waiting for us to invite the movement that will take us to where we want to go.

Our solution to any problem is dependent on the way that we define the problem

I remember watching a hockey practice of small boys who were likely around five years old. At one moment, one of the children got the puck and with great gusto and determination, began to make his way to the net. He was working really hard at staying up on his skates while keeping the puck at least in the vicinity of his stick. As he approached the net, the goal tender was waving madly and desperately trying to block the shot, but to no avail. The puck sailed into the net. That little hockey star was elated! He'd done it! Finally, he'd gotten the puck; managed to stand up all the way down the ice; and actually got the puck into the net. It took great courage for the coach to tell him that he'd just scored on his own team!

Perhaps if we focused less attention on the structure of work, and focused more attention on the structure of the individuals who create work, we'd be further ahead

We've been working very hard for a long time now at 'fixing' work, or the organization, or the corporation, or the department, division, etc. And yet, the kind of experiences we are seeking in our work environments seem to continue to elude us. Maybe we're moving rapidly down the wrong end of the rink. Perhaps if we focused less attention on the structure of work, and focused more attention on the structure of the individuals who create work, we'd be further ahead.

This book is not intended to give you answers. It's intended to encourage you to ask the big questions; to dare to not know and venture forth anyway. It is based on the belief that work/life, with most of our adult lives spent in the workplace, is personal. Very personal. And when I collapse at work, whether emotionally, spiritually or physically, it is a very personal experience - and one that will determine the course of my future and profoundly shape the collective, as well. When we are all doing it, we create work environments that no longer support life. Think of where you work......

The power that we all seek - the sense of being in control of shaping our own destiny - is in the questions, not in the answers. The bigger the question, the more life expands. Small questions make for small movements. Einstein knew that the big questions, especially the ones without answers, are what change the world.

Look inside and not outside for your answers. Life is individual and unique. As I (and you) become more willing and able to fully express myself authentically and without fear or shame; as I flow into an ever-expanding capacity to trust my own uncertainty, my own intuition, my own capacity to move forward without having all the answers; collectively, we begin to create systems (at work, at home, in the community) that are large enough to allow for dissension and difference. I cannot create a system that is greater than my own tolerance for uncertainty. The more unsure I am, the greater my need for control and subsequently, the smaller and tighter the systems I will create, leaving me the illusion of being in control.

Look inside and not outside for your answers

I cannot create a system that is greater than my own tolerance for uncertainty

This book is not intended to prescribe solutions. After all, your life belongs to you. I do know this: the more you ask questions of yourself; the more you become willing to explore your beliefs and values, your desires and passions; the more you become willing to engage your own destiny; and the more you become willing to explore the unspeakable (no rules, no models, no case studies, no answers) the more alive and vibrant you become. As you become more alive, so your own choices and prescriptions become more able to support your life and that of those around you.

Rather than offering a prescriptive approach, I would invite you to ponder for a moment the depth of your own wisdom - already present - which you so quickly abandon to someone else's opinion. Perhaps your own considered opinion is your best prescription for creating a life worth living. Don't take my word for it - try it for yourself.

There is a lot around that tells you how to do it. So, how's it working for you so far? Given the number of books, programs, visual and audio products that have proliferated in the last 15 years, work should, by now, have become a haven of productivity and contribution; a sanctuary of blossoming life and personal vitality, and a wonderland of full expression of the authentic self. Such is not the case. To me, it is a sign of insanity to keep doing the same things, over and over again, expecting to achieve a different result. The same perception, the same context, the same approach will only continue to produce the same results. It's not what's happening that's killing us; it's our commitment to the death – sometimes literally – to pretend that it's NOT, that will ultimately do us in. Personally, I want more in life.

For the vast majority of our lives, we have been taught... no, not a strong enough word... we have been kneaded, shaped, fired and glazed to seek outside of ourselves for guidance, direction and what we have come to call the answers

For the vast majority of our lives, we have been taught... no, not a strong enough word... we have been kneaded, shaped, fired and glazed to seek outside of ourselves for guidance, direction and what we have come to call the answers. We defer to someone or something outside of us as a routine course of action. So routine has it become - so mindless - than we have come to think of it not only as the right way but the only way to do something. The alternative is a frightening one for most of us: figure it out for yourself, make it up as you go along and take responsibility for your own life.

We have been taught to seek our direction and counsel outside ourselves: from our parents; then our teachers, at all levels of education; from our doctors, our ministers and our priests; from our bosses, our colleagues, our neighbors and our friends. We have developed the habit of denying the wisest counsel - our own. We have forgotten the innate power of our own instincts, of our own wants and needs. And worse, we have been taught to fear them as if in mortal combat for control of our very lives. We gratefully give up even trying to figure it out for ourselves.

We have developed the habit of denying the wisest counsel - our own

We have become professionals at abandoning ourselves to collective thought; and have become weak and puerile in our capacity to reason for ourselves and worse yet, in our capacity to act alone. Mindlessly taking on the thoughts of others, without looking outside of what we all already know and believe, results in an inbreeding of thought that, over time, will produce the same effect as genetic inbreeding. However the results have a far more devastating effect since thought is a virus and spreads quickly. Our thoughts can transform our lives instantly! Genetically, it can take several generations.

This book is intended to help you to find the courage to act alone; to ask the very questions that, at the thought of them, cause you to feel a sense of panic and nausea because you don't know. We don't know who we really are versus who we have been taught to believe we are; what we believe versus what we've been taught we should believe; and what we want versus what we have been told we should want.

This book is intended to help you to find the courage to act alone

For close to twenty-five years, I have spent my life in the presence of other people who have known, deep in their bellies, that it's time to ask the bigger questions. People for whom life has lost its meaning, regardless of how many possessions they've acquired or how much money they've hoarded or spent. People for whom vitality, joy and playfulness have become not just faint memories but worse, denied experiences. People for whom getting out of bed on Monday morning, to face yet another barren experience, has become more than they can bear - or are ready to tolerate.

These people are not weak or inept or puny. They are the leaders of tomorrow, daring to carve out a trail for others to follow rather than stay lost in the swamp of their own cynicism, despair and contempt of themselves and others. These are the people who have chosen to ask the bigger questions, the questions without answers. These are the people who often find themselves walking alone. However, as we find the courage to stand alone, we notice that around us are others of like mind - not necessarily in their results or in their directions, but in their intention to think for themselves and to reclaim their birthright to do so.

We have done the best that we know how to do. Now, given what we've learned and what's available for us to know, we have new and different tools to help us not only recognize our own potential but to be able to express it in a different way; to shape a new reality for ourselves, one that supports life - at work, at home and in our communities.

It would have been easier for me *not* to write this book. The time, the effort, the energy and the determination could easily have been directed elsewhere. My hope is that in sharing my thoughts, my experiences and my hard-learned lessons, you will not have to do it the hard way; that you will find something that will cause you to stop… and do something else.

We are not helpless. We are people of dignity, integrity and courage

We are not helpless. We are people of dignity, integrity and courage. We have what it takes to build what we want, using the full extent of our resourcefulness which includes all of who we are – past and present. Our past offers the intelligence that we require in order to embrace more of our own potential, not because we remember the past but because by digesting/metabolizing it, we are transformed. Remembering it does not make us better human beings – evolving from it, does. Without it, there are no lessons learned: no experience, no wisdom and no compassion, for ourselves or for others. Our past is intended to teach us, not to tether us to what was or limit what might become.

In addition to all the things that I am capable of and all that I have accomplished, I am first and most importantly a mother. Everyday, my children are a living reminder of the joy, the delight, the curiosity and the opportunity that are the magnificent birthright of who we are as human beings. They are a living testament to the future - to the possibility of our own becoming as a people. The legacy of who I will have become, from one choice to the next, will greatly shape who they are *capable* of becoming. I am unwilling to stand idly by while they are shaped by systems over which I, as an individual, have little direct control or, for that matter, even affect minutely. I am however, very capable of influencing not only what they think about but more importantly ***how*** they think about those things, and at least contribute to their perception of themselves and the world into which they will expand. I want them to know that the world is round.

The legacy of who I will have become, from one choice to the next, will greatly shape who they are *capable* of becoming

May I prove to have been their mother, their teacher, their student and their friend. May you also be or become your greatest gift to those you love.

FULLY ALIVE

The mind is not a vessel to be filled,
but a fire to be ignited.

- Plutarch -

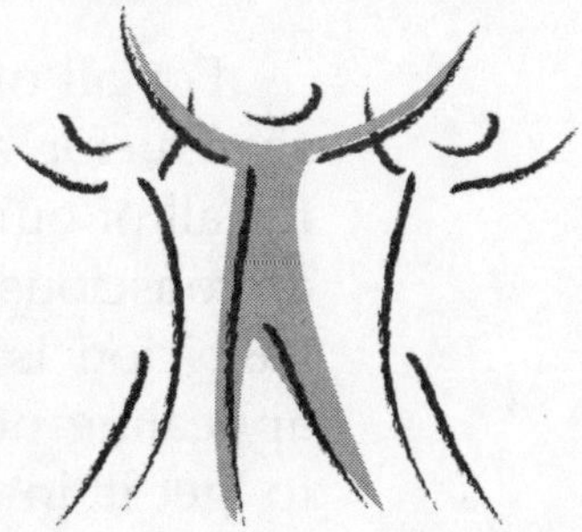

CHAPTER 1

Evolution by Intention™

I am both moved and disturbed by the passage of time and the accompanying realization that not much has really changed. As much as I would like to share with you thoughts that inspire and uplift; thoughts that give the reader a sense of comfort and hope for the unfolding future; thoughts that would likely be more welcomed and in alignment with the expectations of a 'self-help' reader, they simply are not there to be expressed. What is there is recognition that as politically incorrect as it may be, I cannot bring myself to ignore my own observations and pretend otherwise. I am unwilling to ***not*** see what I see, hear what I hear and know what I know.

It may well be that given what many of us already see, we have reached a point in our history where we will not be able to 'OM' away the deeply disturbing trend in the evolution of our humanity and our species. Meditation, prayer, a positive attitude and a deep and abiding faith in a god that will save us all may no longer be sufficient to save us from ourselves. Not because I say so but because the reality we are creating says so. And, like it or not, we are indeed the creators of this reality – and much of it is ugly.

For all of our intensity for and commitment to the search; for all of our willingness and determination; for all of our research and exploration of the evolution of consciousness and advancement of the species, my suspicion is that our report card would not be very appealing nor compelling as evidence of our capacity to 'get it' in a way that allows us to engage differently. We continue to live in a world that appears mindlessly committed to its own demise. Like punching a pillow, just when we think we might have made a difference in one place, we find ourselves bearing witness to another gaping protrusion that has formed itself elsewhere. And on and on it goes, a constant stream of the same problem played out by an endless variety of players, all with the same script. Our willingness, like our hearts, may be in the right place but our ability is lagging pitifully behind.

We continue to live in a world that appears mindlessly committed to its own demise

Like myriad pieces of string rolled into a giant ball, our problems and challenges continue to accumulate and increase in their variety and size, becoming impossible for us not to see. As much as we can discern the color and texture of the threads closest to the surface (planetary upheaval as Gaia manifests her outrage, expressing through increasing density and intensity of earthquakes, hurricanes, tsunamis, mud slides, forest fires; violence toward self and other; decay and collapse at the highest levels of our often decorated and publicly rewarded so-called leadership; political and economic erosion beyond repair; etc.), we continue to be unable to name and claim the ones much closer to the core, allowing the ball to maintain its formation.

We go about our lives, every cell in our body bathed in and formed by the numbing effects of generations of mindless, habituated thinking, asleep to that which crumbles around us, hoping that someone else will take care of it all. What will it take to awaken the giants that we are from the intergenerational slumber that has now become a coma? What will it take for us to call up the courage to find out? Dr. Ervin Laszlo, the founder of systems philosophy, general evolution theory and prolific author of a multitude of ground-breaking books, suggests in his latest offering *The Chaos Point: The World at the Crossroads* (published in 2006) that we have seven years to transform ourselves and our world or face the inevitable and dire consequences of multiple systems in collapse. Not a pretty thought!

For several generations, we have more and more been convinced that we must rely on our intellects to solve our problems. We have surrendered the truth of our personal experiences to the so-called wisdom of the collective believing that in doing so, our needs would be better served. From this approach has come, I believe, the creation of a collective incapable of internal referencing and mindlessly compliant to sets of external directives from the forces that mold and shape who we become (i.e. parenting, education, work, etc.)

We have surrendered the truth of our personal experiences to the so-called wisdom of the collective

We have trained ourselves to look outside of ourselves for guidance and direction; for answers and the 'right' questions, in the hope that somebody, somewhere, would lead us out of the state of decline in which we find ourselves. And here we sit… not just pondering our future but wondering if we will have a future to ponder!

As I write this, I can already see the rolling eyes and hear the murmurs: "Must we do the 'doom and gloom' thing?! Can't we focus on the positive and what's working in the world?!" I'm not suggesting that we should all stop meditating and/or praying and/or anything else we have chosen to do, with the hope of creating change. However, what I am suggesting is that doing so is not occurring on a scale and at a pace that will exceed the existing rate of decline and its increasing momentum. The jury is in: it's not enough.

I wonder inside myself: will we ever find another place to stand? I'm not suggesting that what we have done in the past, to create change, has not had an effect. I am suggesting that in order to affect the change we now require, we must find a new way of engaging that is not an incremental shift in what we know/do but a massive leap into a new way of ***being*** rather than a change in how or what we're ***doing***. The immensity of the problems we face, and their collective and cumulative effect, has moved far beyond our ability to resolve them, no matter how willing we may be, with what we already know and, more importantly, who we have always held ourselves to be. Einstein has already said that the problems of today cannot be resolved at the same level of thinking that created them. It may well be that in raising our level of thinking, we will be required to discover that what must evolve is ***who*** we are as human beings and not just ***how*** or ***what*** we do. Continuing to run the strategies we know and engaging the behaviours that are familiar to us will only get us more of what we've got!

> We must find a new way of engaging that is a massive leap into a new way of being rather than a change in how or what we're doing

It occurs to me that we cannot give away that which does not belong to us. Having said that, I can't let go of my misery until I claim that it's mine to let go of; that it is my own creation; and step fully into it and discover all the genius that it offers, before I can integrate its discoveries into who I can become – so that I might create again, differently.

> We cannot give away that which does not belong to us

This is not a complaint or a plea, it's an invitation. An invitation for us to get honest with ourselves about what works and what doesn't. Truth be told, we already know that and often silence ourselves rather than step fully into the stark terror that comes with this realization. It is an invitation for us to consider what else is there, beyond the old familiar fallback of the intellect, that we might consider as a new approach to problems we have faced throughout the history of mankind. How else might we consider ourselves in relation to these problems such that an awakening occurs – one that allows us to reclaim and engage ourselves in different ways – giving us ***both*** willingness and ability at the same time?

Our intellects aren't working!

- Our intellects aren't working! For how long have we relied on reason and good measure; on the rational, linear thinking way of solving our problems; and on our ability to define a problem, analyze it (which requires that we look back at the 'facts' which are always historical) and then, come to the only reasonable thing to do? As familiar as this approach may be, it's not working. It is linear in nature and the problems we have and continue to create are expanding exponentially.

Our brutality toward the body is not working!

- Our rigor with and brutality toward the body is not working. Our long history of religious requirement to silence the body and defer to dogma is leaving us a people wracked with diseases of the body, mind and spirit. As we continue to do 'the right thing' and deny ourselves what is 'right for' us, we move more steadily into decline. Cut yourself off from your body and you cut yourself off from the truth of your own experience. This schism is essential to our continuing to do what others tell us to do rather than doing what we know is meaningful for us.
- Our willingness to rely on the underlying drive of survival of the fittest is evidence of our mindless belief in random mutation – which we have known for sometime is no longer an absolute 'truth'. Perhaps we stay so committed because we don't know what to do instead.

We stand at a threshold to choose who we will become or prepare ourselves to disappear

I believe we stand at a threshold – a point at which we must mindfully and consciously choose who we will become or prepare ourselves to disappear. Evolution by intention! Not an unfolding based on our past; not an unfolding based on our research and practice and historical preferences but an unfolding based on our having chosen to do so, in a particular way. *Evolution by Intention* stands in an autopoietic framework and recognizes that there is genius in it all; that at the moment of having chosen, it was the right choice to make. The question now is ***not*** "How do we *hold on to* this creation" but becomes "What have we *learned about ourselves from* this creation?" and "Who do we now have the potential to become? " It requires that in moving to levels of thinking beyond that which allowed us to create what has now become the problem, it includes a realization that it is not sufficient to change what we *do*; we must transform who we *are*.

Evolution by Intention does not just require but demands that we recognize that our body is not what we've been taught to believe it is – it is so much more. The human body is not a mechanical device. It is a living, organic, quantum biological processor. And what is it processing? Signals – energy/information that is there for one purpose only and that is to guide us through the process of our own evolution and take us home.

The human body is a living, organic, quantum biological processor

Evolution by Intention demands that we surrender the intellect to the body and let the body lead. As the signals move through the body and the body stabilizes, we come to know both the willingness and the ability to engage for transformation rather than continue to struggle for incremental change.

Evolution by Intention demands that we both recognize and claim the organic nature of the collectives of which we are already a part as well as the ones we anticipate creating. Far more powerful than our existing frameworks of command-and-control is the power of an awakened organic collective and its capacity for contagion. We are powerful beings –living expressions of the god-force in a physical Universe. All we need do is awaken to the truth of our own potential.

Far more powerful is an awakened organic collective and its capacity for contagion

As much as we are perched at a pivotal point in our own evolution, we cannot get there by brushing who we have been under the rug, along with all of its effects. *Evolution by Intention* requires that we stop lying to ourselves and each other; that we uncover and embrace the ugliness of many of our creations and that we claim them, metabolize them and from the genius they carry, become who we are destined to become.

We are running out of time. Not because such is claimed in ancient texts but because our decaying social structures, our imploding educational, corporate and religious systems and the state of wellbeing of our own bodies tell us so. I see what I see, I hear what I hear and I know what I know – and so do you. How much longer can we defer to external references and deny the truth of our own intuitive knowing? We will not evolve by speeding up and going faster and faster, all of which takes us further and further out of and away from the experience of our own bodies. The paradox is that acceleration of consciousness – and its attending evolution – will come from slowing down, re-entering and reclaiming the territory of the body. The only thing you can trust without question is that your body will never lie to you.

The only thing you can trust without question is that your body will never lie to you

The information that follows will show you how to become both willing and able to live differently. In the coming exploration, you will be encouraged to reconsider not only ***who*** you are but ***what*** you are. You'll be invited to reconsider how you got to be who you are; how you think and how that thinking shapes and designs how you live; and what becomes possible when you begin to awaken to the 'more' of who you already are and, more importantly, who you might become. Keep in mind that this is a beginning and much more awaits you when you're ready.

You will also be invited to take those new insights and discoveries into consideration as you redesign your life. Who you are in this moment may feel very different from who you'll have become by the end of the book. As you engage your life in this way, you'll begin to discover that you are much more than you ever dreamed possible – and it all comes from discovering that your body is not the enemy. You can relax into and trust your body to gently guide you home.

So, take heart! Stop for a moment... take a nice, long, slow, deep breath... and step gently into your future, ready to discover the amazing Being that you are! You are not alone on this journey. As you decloak and allow others to know of your curiosity and your search, you'll find yourself in good company.

You are not alone on this journey

As you move into the following chapters, may you find within yourself the courage and the willingness to live every day awake and aware, choosing a meaningful life over a familiar one. From one breath to the next, the time is *now*.

FULLY ALIVE

It is not what we don't know that causes us problems.
It is what we are so sure we do know that just ain't so.

- Mark Twain -

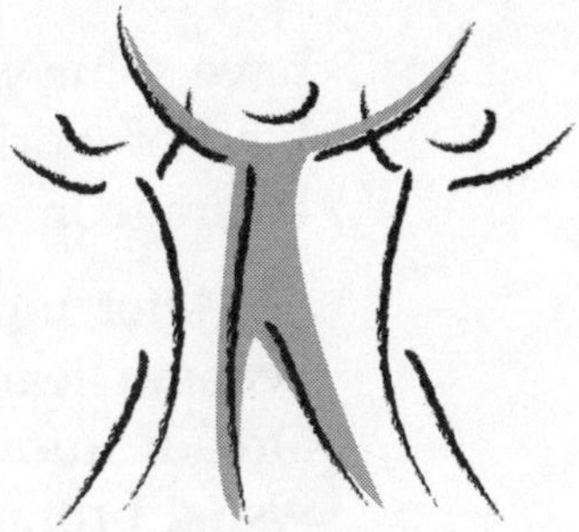

CHAPTER 2

The Journey

What's this all about?

As adults, we spend more time at work than we spend anywhere else in our lives. For at least five days out of seven, we go to a place where we do something for which we are paid. Many of us then take this money and do something else that we call living: buy things, take trips, plan holidays, pay bills, spend time with people we enjoy. But few of us ever consider the possibility that work isn't something that we do, or a place that we go to. It's an experience that we create and often times, the experience is not a pleasant one. Given that we spend more waking time at work than anywhere else, imagine the profound results on our quality of life if we were to make a significant change in the way we experience work. The potential is life-altering.

As children, school is the 'work' of our youth. We are required to be part of a collective process that is designed for us by the adults that surround us with the intention that the context for and the design of our education will serve the needs of the collective when we become old enough to enter the workforce. At least as adults, we have some sense of choice over where we work and the kind of work that we do. As children, we have no such leverage in our own lives.[1]

After more than 40 years in the work force, it has become clear to me that work isn't working. But then, you already know that. Just think of all the books, audio and visual products, seminars and workshops on the topic of work: organizational change, organizational renewal, learning organizations, team building, organizational spirituality… and on it goes. For the past three decades, we have been aware that something is amiss and have been working diligently to do something about it. And yet, even with all that desire and intention, even with all that information and intelligence, work still isn't working for far too many of us.

We now have more than enough evidence to indicate that to continue to approach the issues of work from the level of thinking at which we've been operating isn't going to get us where we want to go. Perhaps it's time for us to *redirect* our thinking *away from the content* of work (i.e. the where, when and what of work, meaning the physical environments we work in and the tasks of the work, as well as all the structures, practices, policies, procedures and strategies) and begin to direct attention *toward the context* that we've created for work that has become a habit of thinking and transparent to us as the workers.

It's time for us to notice that work isn't a place we go to or something that we do. Work, like life, is an experience that we have that is of our own creation, based on the way we think: about ourselves, about our world and about our capacity to function in that world.

---

1 For more thoughts on the educational system, see *When the Horse Dies, Get Off… and Stop Dragging It Around!*

If we were to take the time to notice, we might begin to recognize that how we engage work is a metaphor for how we engage life!

The *context* of work invites much larger questions than the *content* and does not lend itself so easily to statistical, quantifiable data. The context of work is related to the bigger issue of the box in which we have placed work for several generations and then scrutinized what's inside. It is related to the way we have defined work and simply assume that we know exactly what it is, and so does everyone else. Since all meaning is context dependent, it will serve us well to devote some attention to the context of work and begin to explore and possibly redefine what we hold work to be. Maybe we should begin by looking at the box itself.

Think back to the days of Christopher Columbus. There was a time when we thought that the world was flat. Within this world-view (or context), travel was a dangerous thing. Move too close to the horizon and you could drop off the edge of the world! The belief that the world was flat brought with it limitations and dangers that simply vanished when we changed our minds. When we came to believe that the world was round (and it was nothing more than a change of mind since the 'facts' had not changed) life expanded in a burst of movement. Commerce exploded; cultures migrated; things once held to be impossible soon became a way of life. All that, just because we changed our minds.

What if, in the world of work/life, we believe we are living in a flat world? What if that world isn't really flat and its limitations are of our own creation? What if the world of work is really round and holds the potential to invite and nurture health, humor, compassion and truth? What if it's not your work/life that holds you back

Change your mind and you change your life

but your own context for thinking about it? Imagine the alternatives if you were to change your mind. Change your mind and you change your life.

What it's *not* about!

This isn't really a book about work; it's a book about life – your life and mine. It just so happens that we'll spend more of our lives "at work" than we'll spend anywhere else. Given the impact of this reality simply by virtue of time invested, when work doesn't work neither does life. However, my belief is that focusing all that attention on work is a red herring; a way of keeping us occupied and feeling like we're doing something useful when, in fact, we're not.

Trying to use work to leverage change in our life experience is like putting the cart in front of the horse and then beating the horse because it's not moving fast enough! I think we'd get further, faster, if instead of focusing our attention on the cart and/or the horse, we began to pay attention to how we had coupled them… *to the process* we had designed and within which we considered them. It's not that the horse isn't ready to get on with it; it's that we've designed it in a way that makes it really tough to get on with it.

This isn't a book about improving business practices or changing organizational structures. It's about feelings; about creating work environments – emotional, energetic and behavioral environments – that allow us to come to life during the multitude of hours that we spend at work; to be authentic, to be honest, to have compassion; to be able to be unsure and still be perceived as intelligent and committed and dedicated. Unlike many other books that address the topic of work, this book is not about statistics and quantifiable information. What could I possibly add along this line of thinking – at this level of thinking - that would make a difference? What could

I say that would be news, given that you already work somewhere and know better than anyone else what your experience is. My approach is highly qualitative and subjective but then, isn't that what the experience of work is all about?

It's not about case studies. Although there is always much to be learned from our history and the history of others, case studies are stories that we tell in hopes of discovering the moral by which to live differently. Story telling can be informative and entertaining, and may even invite incremental change. However, if you're looking for 'transformation', you can only find that inside… where you live. My invitation to you is to stand fully in the present and allow history to wash over you (as uncomfortable as that may prove to be); metabolize and/or integrate the genius that it offers and step boldly into the future of your choosing.[2]

If you're looking for 'transformation', you can only find that inside… where you live

It's not another 'how to' book, giving you the answers and telling you what to do. As tempting as it may be for me to assume that my best choices may also be yours, I'll leave that up to you. We have become junkies for the 'Ten Steps to...' and 'The Five Keys to...'. Once you've had an opportunity to develop a greater sense of mindfulness about how you've defined the 'problem', you'll know exactly 'how to' proceed (for you) in order to make a difference in your life.

It's not about generalizing to provide you with a formula for relating to the people you work with and spend time with so you can assume that now, you *really* know how *they* are. Given that human beings are quantum biological beings, they are not ever the same from one moment to the next (more about that later).

2 For more, see Quantum TLC™ in *Phoenix Rising: The Freeing of Human Potential*.

It's not the work of an expert. I have neither Ph.D. nor am I the hardened CEO of a multi-national corporation or a university professor whose practice includes business and organizational systems. That I am not these does not mean that I don't see what I see, hear what I hear and know what I know. Like you, I've spent most of my life working. And, like you, I'm nobody's fool. I know what truth feels like inside me, just like I can recognize deception. I know what makes for a sense of contribution and accomplishment; and I know what it feels like to be on the outside looking in, not even sure that I want to be in but feeling badly about being left out. This book is written intentionally for the 'average' person – the curious, sensing and aware person. It's written with an unshakable belief that underneath the veneer of the job title, or lurking behind the details of a job description, we are first and foremost human. What I have written is not for your intellect or your logic or your analysis; it's for your gut, your heart and your soul.

I know what truth feels like inside me, just like I can recognize deception

What I have written is not for your intellect or your logic or your analysis; it's for your gut, your heart and your soul

This book is not intended to give you solutions. It is intended to invite inquiry into elements of work you may never have considered, ways of thinking that may have (until now) escaped you and to press the edges of your own belief structures – about you and about the people around you.

As you read through this material, you may not always feel good. This book is not about work, as we consider it to be 'out there'. It's about work as we have created it from 'in here'. That means that it's personal and it's about how we live. As you proceed through the material, you will be invited to come face-to-face with yourself. What you do with that is entirely up to you. My suggestion to you would be that as you go through the book, pay attention to your breathing. Notice when you begin to hold your breath or begin to breathe very shallowly from the top of the lungs. When you notice, take a moment to sit back, take a couple of deep breaths and relax. Focus your attention on letting your belly soften, your shoulders drop and your arms hang loose by your sides. When the truth inside you begins to move, use your breathing to give it the space it requires to come to life.

Who's it for?

Given that you're reading this book, it is fairly safe to assume that you're looking for something. Either you have a sense that something is missing or you have a sense that there is something else available to you that will make a difference in the quality of your life and the lives of the people you work or live with.

It may be useful for you to know that this book is intended to share information with you, not tell you what to do or how to live or what choices to make. (Without new information, we are destined - some might say 'doomed' - to have the same conversation the same way, over and over again, feeling lucky if we manage to get even the slightest change in results! We've learned to settle for crumbs.) For that reason, we've intentionally allowed for lots of room in the margins for you to jot down your thoughts and reactions as you move through the material. The power is not in the content of the book - it's in what the content evokes in <u>you</u>. Write down your thoughts and insights as they surface.

The power is in what the content evokes in you

Your life belongs to you, not me. The intention is to present information in such a way that you will be drawn to it: to ask questions that you may not yet have thought of and offer them to you for consideration, with you making choices for yourself all along the way. If something appeals to you – great! If not, let it go and move on. There are no rules about how to read the book, either. Start anywhere you'd like and move to where you want to go. Let the topics that interest you most call to you first.

One of the presuppositions about life that I live by is that there are no accidents in the Universe; that everything unfolds exactly as it should. This means that whatever my experience, it has a purpose. I can complain about my life or I can ask different questions, like: what is there for me to learn from this experience? Or, what is there for me to learn *about myself* from this experience? These assumptions, which have guided and served me for some time now, may be worth exploring.

I can complain about my life or I can ask different questions

I've also made some basic assumptions about you, as a reader, which have guided and directed both my approach and the degree to which I have simply stated what's true for me without caution and caveat. Some of them are as follows:

- You are not broken, deficient or dysfunctional. The work, family and community environments that we have created and participate in are a natural by-product of the things that we have been taught. Expand what we know and life expands with it.
- You are already doing the best you know how to do. Given your beliefs, values and attitudes, and given the information you have and the context within which you operate, you are already doing what you believe is available or possible or best for you to do.
- You already have what you need in order for you to create the quality of life at work and elsewhere that you want for yourself. You are already intelligent and resourceful. The question is not whether the resources are there; the challenge is whether or not you can get at them. The purpose of this book is to help you to be able to rediscover this information and put it to use in your day-to-day living.

- You know better than any one else what's good for you. What you choose to do with your life is up to you. For me to prescribe solutions would diminish your own potential.
- You have a brilliant mind with unlimited potential for making choices that support and sustain life. Although you may have forgotten how to use it, it is neither missing nor inoperative.
- And finally, I believe that it is your nature to grow and to expand. I believe that the nature of being human is to participate and contribute. It is our nature to create. It is impossible for us to do otherwise.

Although this book uses your experience of work, its approach is different in that it is written for you as a human being, first and foremost. Regardless of your function within those larger systems – corporate leader, clerk, manager, doctor, administrator, waiter – you are first and foremost human. We've forgotten that and it shows. The information in this book will serve you as an individual and will also make a difference in the way you approach your experience of work and your experience with your colleagues/clients.

You are first and foremost human. We've forgotten that and it shows

The great leveler is that there is nothing going on at work but individual human beings interacting with other individual human beings. Sometimes these interactions take place by phone or email; sometimes in formal meetings and sometimes over lunch or coffee; and sometimes they take place through a circulation of information through documents: policies, plans, strategies or minutes. But nevertheless, each is a way of moving the thoughts/notions/ideas of one through the minds of many. For this reason, it becomes important to understand that within the individual human being, there are always two conversations going on: the one you have with yourself and the one you subsequently have with another human being. Here's the trick: you

The great leveler is that there is nothing going on at work but individual human beings interacting with other individual human beings

Here's the trick: you can't change the conversation you have with another human being unless and until you are both willing and able to change the one you have with yourself – first

can't change the conversation you have with another human being unless and until you are both willing and able to change the one you have with yourself – *first*.

That conversation you have inside yourself dictates the degree to which you will express your 'truth' to another human being: what you'll say, how you'll say it and the degree to which it will be clear, direct, open and honest. For example, let's say I've just hired you to redecorate my house. Although I hate the color blue, it's very 'in' right now and trendy: you and my friends are really big on the color blue. When you ask me about color, I tell you that I like blue. That becomes one of the driving considerations in the plan that you subsequently develop. How much do you think I'm going to like what you've done? How much of it did I create for myself? Who am I likely to be annoyed with – you or me; or both?

If the conversation you are having with yourself is that the other person/people won't understand or support you, your revelations will be guarded and positioned accordingly. If the conversation you have with yourself is that the other person/people will be open to hearing your ideas, your approach will be very different. And why would any of this matter? Because in the things we say and do – or don't – we literally structure our personal reality and the reality we share with others. If we are not telling what is true for us, then what we tell is untrue. This untruth then creates environments that are illusions - not real, imaginary, made up. There is no great mystery to why we don't get what we want. And all of this starts inside you first. How well does any of us know what's going on inside of ourselves let alone have any understanding of what's going on inside another human being?

If we are not telling what is true for us, then what we tell is untrue. This untruth then creates environments that are illusions

How will this make a difference?

You can't get where you're going until you know where you are. If you ask me for directions on how to get to Hawaii, it would matter whether you were in Vancouver or Auckland. We can't create work/life environments that support and sustain life until we understand where we are now and how we got that way. We are the creators of our own experience through the things we say and do – and the things we won't say and won't do. In moving our thinking to a higher level when considering work, we create the opportunity to begin to notice that perhaps we have missed the forest given our preoccupation with the trees.

We are the creators of our own experience through the things we say and do

As we move our attention away from the content of work (the where, when and what of work) and begin to consider work from a context perspective, we become curious about different things and begin to ask a different set of questions, such as: Who am I at work? How does who I am at work and who I am elsewhere fit together? How does my identity as an individual overlap with the identity of my organization? These are much larger questions, which tend not to have easily quantifiable answers.

I believe that the quality of my life is not dependent on the accuracy of my answers but on the courage of my questions. It takes a lot of courage to be willing to entertain the questions that do not have easy answers and perhaps, do not yet have any answers at all! Einstein knew this. In his willingness to trust himself and venture forth, the experience of those big, courageous questions he asked himself - allowing himself to think the unthinkable - profoundly altered the world in which we live.

The quality of my life is not dependent on the accuracy of my answers but on the courage of my questions

For more than twenty years, we've been asking small questions. We've learned. We've grown. We've changed. We are now at a place and in a time when we are ready for the bigger questions; for the ones that don't necessarily have answers but in the asking alone, we will expand the way we live.

Cause and effect

In the *cause/effect* expression of life, *cause* is a more powerful place to stand. For many of us, our experience of work is that we are at the *effect* of (or victim to) the system. Being at the effect of something implies that we are without the capacity to choose; without the ability to cause something to take place and are at the mercy of the choice someone else has made. The capacity to choose implies the presence of power. And yet, the power is not in the choice itself but in the process of the choosing.

Power is not in the choice itself but in the process of the choosing

Power does not reside in the end result of the choice but in the ability to choose again, and again and again, allowing each subsequent choice to reflect new information, new experience and new wisdom. We sometimes make choices and then believe that we must now live forever with that choice; that we cannot change our minds and choose again or choose differently. And yet, movement is a sign of life. Each subsequent choice allows for the movement that is required in order for us to get on with our lives, to grow and to create new things to experience. Without movement, there is no indication of the presence of life. Without movement, things eventually die. With the power of choice comes the experience of creating. With the power of *conscious* choice comes the awareness that we have always been creating and can choose to create again with intention and restructure our worlds.

With the power of choice comes the experience of creating; with the power of conscious choice comes the awareness that we have always been creating

What we will explore in subsequent chapters is that we are not victims. Nor are we powerless and helpless in the face of these larger living systems we call work, organizations or corporations. We are profoundly powerful and are creating our own experience of work/life from moment to moment to moment. We are always at cause in our experience and we are always choosing. The question is: are we choosing mindfully? Are we choosing with a sense of purposefulness? Or do we just keep doing what we know how to do or what everyone else is doing or thinks we should be doing? Are we choosing mindlessly and simply allowing habit to run its course?

We are always at cause in our experience and we are always choosing. The question is: are we choosing mindfully?

Many people feel powerless in their work/life experience. In defining power as the capacity to produce an intended result, it may be helpful to notice that the choices you've already made have produced a result called the quality of your life. How do you like it so far? The useful questions to ponder are not whether what you've already created is good or bad, right or wrong. The more powerful question is: is it useful? Does it serve you? Will it get you where you want to go? If not, you may want to give some thought to creating something else.

The useful questions to ponder are not whether what you've already created is good or bad, right or wrong. The more powerful question is: is it useful?

Be aware that it is impossible for you NOT to create. Every thought you think, every word you say and all of your behaviors produce a result. Ask yourself: "What am I building?" If you were to think of each result or experience as a brick in the construction of your dream, what is it that's unfolding before your very eyes? And is that what you want?

Where to from here?

A wise woman once said: "When the horse dies, get off!!" Good advice, I'd say. And yet, when it comes to creating work environments that support life, we keep trying to ride the same dead horse. We continue to seek movement from something that has no life. We approach work as if it is something that exists 'out there'; something that is separate from who I am; something that is an act of the intellect and the conscious mind; and something that can be solved through analysis, willpower and determination. We keep beating a dead horse.

If we keep doing what we're doing, we'll get more of what we've got

As we raise our level of thinking about work and explore what work is, we find that we must go into deeper levels of mind. Higher levels of thinking necessitate deeper levels of mind. We aren't going to get where we want to go the way we've always been trying to get there. We've forgotten that if we keep doing what we're doing, we'll get more of what we've got. You'll notice that the fundamental issues about work have not changed much in the last 30 years. They are still about feeling disrespected, irrelevant, dismissed and marginalized; feeling unseen and unheard. How this gets expressed is through absenteeism, illness, strikes, demands for more money and an increased level of activity in Employee Assistance Program (EAP) requirements. Not to mention the rise in the use of drugs, both prescription and otherwise. Maybe it's time we found another way. Better yet, maybe it's time for us to invent one!

I do not believe that we, as people, are dysfunctional. Nor do I believe that our society or our behaviors are dysfunctional. I believe that what we are experiencing is a predictable byproduct of our own creation, given the way we raise our children and behave with each other. They are further reinforced by powerful, culturally ingrained processes that include the first and most significant – parenting. Add to parenting the conditioning processes of religion, school and work, mindful that the first two of these fall into the category of 'sacred, untouchable and not-to-be-questioned', and you have the ingredients for a seamless progression into a structured and habituated 'reality'.

Changing the recipe

The situation we find ourselves in today is not a result of something gone wrong - it's the consistent result of something gone according to plan. Think of it this way: if you have a recipe for brownies and you diligently follow that recipe, what comes out of the oven is brownies. If what you want is banana bread and yet you continue to follow the recipe for brownies because that's the one you know – the one that you can easily find and have had success with in the past – why would you be surprised when brownies comes out of the oven? What's the point in berating the brownies because you wanted banana bread? What will you accomplish by complaining about the brownies, the depth of color of the chocolate, the fact of nuts or no nuts, when what you really want is banana bread? Doesn't it make more sense to change the recipe?

The situation we find ourselves in today is not a result of something gone wrong - it's the consistent result of something gone according to plan

We've now reached a point where we no longer want what we're getting. For years, we've been making adjustments to the brownie recipe with the end result being brownies, nonetheless. It might be useful to revisit the plan/recipe. Blaming the recipe won't make a difference. Changing it, will!

The destination

We've been trying for a long time to change our experience of work/life. What I am suggesting to you and will be exploring with you in the coming pages is that trying to change work by focusing our attention on work is like trying to figure out what David Copperfield (magician/illusionist) is doing by putting our attention on the airplane (note: he makes a full-sized jet disappear off a stage!). That's not where the point of leverage is - that's where the effect is. If you want to change the result, you have to know what David Copperfield knows.

I believe in building dynamic, living organic collectives (organizations/communities/families, etc) through powerful people – one person at a time. I believe in the power of *one!* I also know how contagious thought is. We live with it all the time, only we've come to know it as gossip or the 'rumor mill'. Imagine the potential for change that lies waiting for us in a better understanding of the power of our own thoughts – as a system – and our ability to engage that system with focus and intention. I know that as you come to terms with that within yourself, the effects upon the systems in which we live our lives are exponential.

Work/life is really one thing – you

What we'll explore in the coming pages is that work/life is really one thing – you. If you want to change your experience of work/life, it can only happen as a by-product of changing yourself, first. We have made work the equivalent of the stage play that we enact on a daily basis, with each of us playing our role. When the play ends, we soak up the applause for yet another performance and then leave the theater to go home to our lives. The only problem is, we've come to believe that the characters we play are real; that we have no choice but to play that character; and that we are trapped in performing in this play, forever. We've forgotten that we developed the play and wrote the scripts. What we once owned now owns us. We have allowed ourselves to be taken hostage by the constructs of our own mind… taken hostage by our own creations.

We are the ones who have dichotomized work and life. We are the ones who have made work the bigger chunk of reality, as opposed to having work fit into the larger context of our lives, as a natural expression of that life. We're beginning to notice the effects of that now and are looking for ways to "balance" work and life. Perhaps it's not so much about balance but is instead about integration, wholeness and alignment. Perhaps it requires that we take two things that we hold as separate and bring them together in a way that creates an entirely new third experience; where the whole becomes greater than the sum of the parts.

Perhaps it's not so much about balance but is instead about integration, wholeness and alignment

Maybe what we're looking for is a way to create an experience of work/life that makes room for consistency of authentic expression, allowing us to be genuine and to be truthful from 9 to 5, too. Maybe what we really want and what many are now moving to with the advent of technology and home-based businesses, is to bring the expression of work back into the fold of living an authentic life. How do we do that?

What we really want is to bring the expression of work back into the fold of living an authentic life

The approach

The approach will encompass four distinct phases: Naming It, Claiming It, Choosing It and Changing It.

The process of *Naming It* has already been well-explored in many other works. The difference is that I will be defining the problem from a different perspective, given my personal experience as an employee in organizational systems as well as from my experience from having worked with people from these systems for more than 25 years. This process helps us to put some structure to what we currently would call 'reality' and our experience of it. *Naming It* is affixing a label and telling the story of what the label describes.

Claiming It is essential to letting something go. You can't give away what doesn't belong to you; nor can you 'renovate' what isn't yours. Unless we can claim what we've created, we are destined to live at the mercy of its expression, assuming that someone/something else is the creator and we are victim to its whims. This part of the process may not always feel comfortable, as we have been brought up to feel such intense responses to that which we judge as broken or wrong or dysfunctional. Do keep in mind my belief that we are always doing the best we know how to do. What's missing is new information to make it possible for us to do something else.

Consciously *Choosing It* is a requirement for a happy ending. Before leaving on a trip, it's wise to know where you want to go. Likewise, before we can begin to change our current experience, we would be well advised to know what we want to experience instead and choose mindfully. Not a knee-jerk response so that we can feel like we're doing something but a considered, intentional, conscious choice; one that we've explored and are moving into with our eyes wide open.

And finally, *Changing It*. What are the tools of behavior, thought and spirit that we can use to rebuild, or to build in a new way? What is our context for taking this action? What are the processes that will not only produce the result we want but that will keep the process alive so that change continues naturally as a way of manifesting life? You'll be introduced to Quantum TLC™ as a provocative and compelling way to engage the truth of your own experience and invite it to work for you instead of against you.

Think of it in terms of a trip. We've already taken a trip, perhaps one that we're no longer very fond of. Seemed like a good idea at the time, and given what we knew and what resources we had available to us, it was the right choice. Now, we have gained the experience of having taken the trip and we are wiser than we were when we began.

The trip has altered and shaped who we have become. We now have the opportunity to either spend the rest of our lives complaining about that trip: about what we coulda/shoulda/woulda done or finding who's wrong for having taken that trip and finding someone to blame; or we can learn from the experience and travel once more. This time, we may want to include in the choosing of our destination more information about who we've become and what appeals to us now, our current resource levels and the intention of the trip. Once we decide that, we can figure out how we're going to get there, mindful that the journey itself - and not just the destination - is a large part of the enjoyment of the experience of any trip.

Figure 1 offers a context for approaching these four phases. Consider for a moment that the circle represents the domain of all knowledge. That means that everything you now know, everything you have ever known and anything that you could ever possibly know in the future, are all contained within this circle. If you were to identify the part of the circle that represents what you know you already know (for example, I know that I know my name; I know that I know how many children I have, where I live, etc.), it would be represented by the first small slice of the pie. If you were then to identify what you know you don't know (say, for example, I know that I don't know a lot about statistics, or scuba diving, or rock climbing – but I know that those things exist and that there are many other people who know a lot about those things), that would be represented by the second small slice of the pie inside the circle. What remains represents everything that I don't know that I don't know. For example, I may not know that I don't know that my body produces a new stomach lining every six days, but that does not mean that it's not happening! Nor does it mean that there aren't many other people who already know this. The fact that I don't know that I don't know those things does not mean that I am not profoundly shaped and affected by them.

Figure 1: Structure of Reality

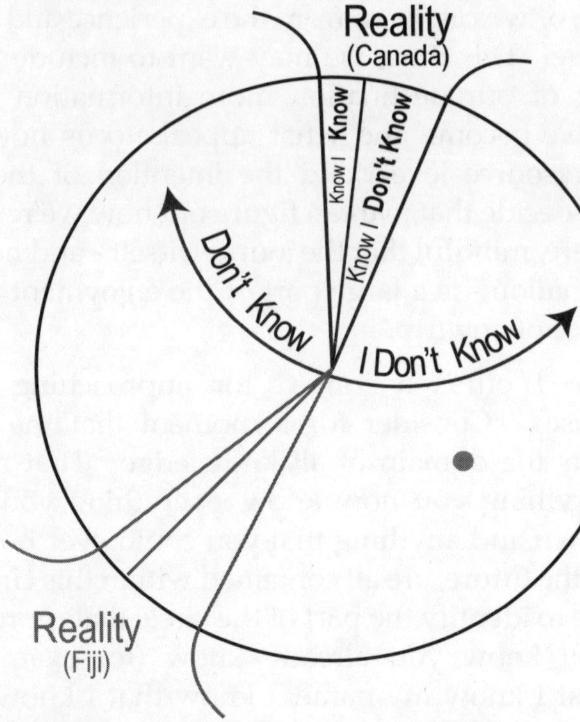

CREATIVITY INNOVATION EMPOWERMENT CHANGE

The biggest chunk of the pie – what you don't know you don't know – holds the greatest potential. The first two small slices we have come to call 'reality' or 'truth'. Those are the things we already know and therefore assume to be real or fact. We often live our lives within the confines of these small, tight spaces because they are familiar and afford the illusion of control. Even when faced with an experience that challenges the structure of that reality, we frequently choose the structure and dismiss the experience, sealing our fate to constantly repeat what we already know.

That vast, unexplored, undefined chunk that represents what we don't even know we don't know, is really where all potential resides. If we say we want creativity and innovation, we have no choice but to go to that vast empty space. Creativity, by definition, means bringing into existence something that does not already exist. You won't find that in the first two small slices – you've already got that! If you want creativity and innovation; if you want authentic and profound change, you have got to go into that unexplored territory. To attempt to create change from our existing structures of reality will produce the illusion of change (i.e. a temporary sense of movement) but it will not alter the structure of our existence. Albert Einstein knew that and now we do, too.

If you want creativity and innovation; if you want authentic and profound change, you have got to go into that unexplored territory

As we become willing to step into 'what we don't know we don't know', the structure of our 'reality' begins to expand. The slice of the pie that is my world, as I know it, begins to grow. As it grows, so does my capacity to engage things that once were outside my comfort zone, or my frame of reference, or my worldview. As my worldview or my context expands, so does my life.

What we typically have referred to as 'diversity' issues are more readily understood when explored within the structure of this model. If I grow up and am conditioned into the 'reality' of Canada and its values and attitudes, and you grow up in Fiji in its reality and values and attitudes, we likely will not experience the world the same way. Does that mean that my way is right and yours is wrong? Or does it just mean that you know things I don't, have beliefs and values and attitudes that are different from mine, and that everything you do makes perfect sense to you in the structure of your reality. The more I expand my thinking – meaning, the more information I have that adds to my existing base of what's real for me – the greater the opportunity for my reality to overlap with yours. The more informed I become, the more flexible I am in communicating with you in your structures of reality. The person with the greatest flexibility of behavior and world-view will ultimately drive (or influence) the system(s) within which he/she operates.

In the pages that follow, you will be invited to step into what you don't know that you don't know. Given our cultural conditioning, this is sometimes a frightening place to be and with very good reason. Stepping into this vast space that is teeming with potential sometimes has attached to it the fears that go along with not knowing: making a mistake, being wrong or being laughed at. What also goes along with this experience is the capacity to shape the very structure of our experience and hence the quality of our lives. The journey will not be a dull one!

For more information, consider:

- *Evolution's End* by Joseph Chilton Pearce
- *Beyond the Quantum* by Michael Talbot
- *The Self-Aware Universe* by Amit Goswami
- *The Seat of the Soul* by Gary Zukav
- *Creation Spirituality* by Matthew Fox
- *The Field* by Lynne McTaggart

FULLY ALIVE

If you want to change your life, you must first change the way that you perceive your life.

-Trick of the Light-

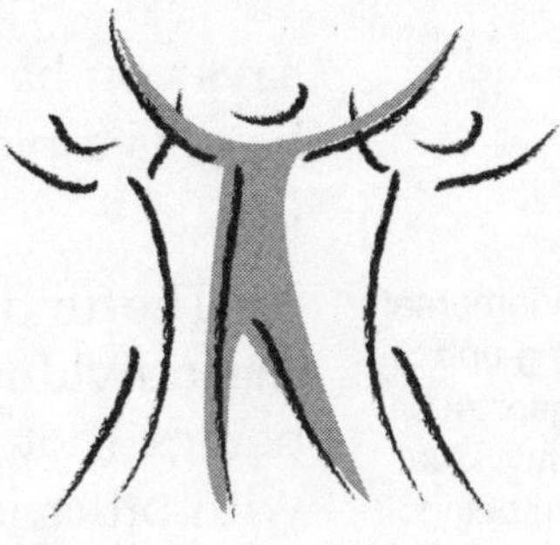

CHAPTER 3

Naming It

What is work?

Typically, when you ask people to think about work, certain things come to mind. They'll think about the building they go to or the office they sit in. They'll think about the commute and the road they take or the bus they ride. They'll think about the last meeting they had and how they did or didn't get what they wanted. Sometimes they'll think about the list of things they have to do, or the report that's not written, or the delivery that didn't get made. They may even think about their technology and the way it makes their lives better or not. But whatever they think about, it tends to be done in a way that positions work 'out there'; away from and distinctly separate from them as individuals and certainly not as a part of who they are. 'Work' is a place they go to that is separate from them and requires that they do something different from their 'real lives'.

Here's a simple truth about work: you can take all the people at your place of work and move them somewhere else, and work will still exist. You can put those people in different jobs, or different offices and work will still exist. You can take away technology or upgrade technology, and work will still exist. But if you send everyone home, and you don't hire anyone else, work will cease to exist. You may have a document that says you have an incorporated company, but what you have is a piece of paper with words on it. There is no life.

The fundamental operating unit of any organization is the individual human being

The fundamental operating unit of any organization is the individual human being. Without individual human beings (not resources or groups or teams) interacting with other individual human beings (one-on-one or in groups, face-to-face or via paper or technology), the organization ceases to exist. Work is nothing more than a collective of individuals, coming together with the intention to produce a particular product or service. As each of these individual living systems come together with other individual living systems, we create larger living systems that are a reflection of the individuals that created it.

In today's science, there are references to particles that are so small they are beyond the capacity of our instrumentation to detect. Although they defy measurement directly, they can be recognized and named because of the distinct particle trail they leave behind, like a footprint or a signature. The 'particle trail' that we leave behind in organizational systems that is the evidence of our presence or effect and that allows us to be defined is what we call a corporate culture. The corporate culture is not a thing on its own. It is a reflection of something else, with that something else being the internal states of the human beings who have created it.

The corporate culture is not a thing on its own. It is a reflection of the internal states of the human beings who have created it

Work is very, very personal. And yet, we continue to kid ourselves into thinking that work is 'out there'; that it requires us to be objective and detached and 'professional'. Truth is, there is nothing more subjective and personal that the day-to-day operations of any living system.

Not only is work a living system, but every living system is connected to every other living system. The family system does not exist in isolation of the community system or the work system or the educational system. Each of these systems feeds into every other system, both affecting and being affected by each other. Is there any wonder that what's happening in our work environments is also what's happening in our schools and communities?

Where are we now?

Before you can move on to where we want to be, we must first know where we are: our point of departure or the platform on which we stand to take our first step into our journey. Before we can move on to create work/life environments that invite health, humor, compassion and truth, we must first stop – and pay attention to where we are now, to what we now have, to what we have created, to what we are now living with that is the legacy of the choices we have made to this point. Taneo Sands Kumalai once said: "In life, nothing is free. For all things, you must pay… attention." We must first get a good sense of the 'brownies'.

Let's take a look at what it's like to go to work today. Just for a moment, imagine yourself about to get out of bed on Monday morning and get ready to go to work. What does it feel like inside you, knowing that the weekend is over and that you now face another five days? Can you hardly wait to get up and at 'em, or do you find yourself rolling over for just another ten minutes? Do you find that your mind leaps into gear with the thoughts of all the wonderful things that you will do today or this week? Or is it your stomach that leaps into gear and begins to churn at the thought of going back?

Once you get to work, ask your buddies what it's like for them to get up on Monday morning and know that they are heading back to 'the salt mines'; or, if you have staff, put this question ahead of the agenda and then watch the body language. Watch for the shuffling in the seats or the rolling of the eyes; and listen for the snickers and the giggles. Watch as people look around the room at each other, knowingly, since they'll likely think the question is some kind of trap, a way of catching them with the wrong attitude or a negative outlook. There is much to be learned about our work environments from this one, small question.

We barely understand our own feelings and what to do with them, let alone what to do with anyone else's

We are frequently unwilling to ask this question because not only is it personal, we often don't have a clue how to deal with the truth of the response once we get it. We have been taught that people's feelings are personal and don't belong at work. Not only that, we barely understand our own feelings and what to do with them, let alone what to do with anyone else's. And yet, who amongst us does not know – deep in the belly – the enormity of the power of these emotions? Who amongst us does not go out of our way to avoid, or worse to "make nice with" these emotions when they surface in our presence? And who amongst us would have the courage to wonder: what would life be like if we could learn to embrace these emotions; to own them rather than have them own us; and to harness the power and redirect this vital force to build and create? It is far easier for us to fix a business plan or adjust a strategy than it is for us to confront an uncomfortable experience.

We have no idea what to do with 'uncomfortable experiences' which occur inside us and do not easily lend themselves to quantifiable data. And yet, the truth of these experiences for the people who are having them is akin to the canaries in the mines. Without a capacity to recognize, value and respond to their messages, our environments move into deeper and deeper states of decline that do not support and sustain life.

We've now been working at reworking the organization for a very, very long time. Some of the best and brightest minds in the world - people like Peter Drucker, Edwards Demming and more recently Tom Peters, Stephen Covey and Peter Senge – have focused and continue to focus their attention on making work a place that supports and sustains life: a place where people want to be and are willing to stay, and one that allows for participation and contribution. Yet, for all this great intention and intellectual elegance, ordinary people within the rank and file of organizational systems do not feel energized, revitalized and ready to rock and roll!

By now, we must have noticed and be asking ourselves: how come? Given the preponderance to devote time and space to this topic, it speaks highly of the degree to which it pervades the culture and the degree to which it touches us profoundly and personally, since we spend more waking time at work than anywhere else in our lives.

Our children have their own workplaces - school

Our children have their own workplaces – school. Look what's happening there! Their 'work environments' are no more life sustaining than our own. Many schools have become war zones, with kids being frisked for weapons when they come through the doors. At a less extreme, schoolyards are often the arena in which the local bullies get to demonstrate their prowess with the teachers often standing by and clucking 'boys will be boys', as other children are pummeled into states of physical pain and emotional terror. What's it like for *our children* to get out of bed on Monday morning and go to 'work'? Our children rely on us to create their systems for them. What have we created for our kids that they must now live out, day after day?

Have we created systems that support and encourage the evolution of their own potential or have we created systems that are designed to mold and shape them into what we think they should become – just like us? The incidences of emotional and physical violence in the school experience are increasing. Perhaps we will become willing to do for our children what we have not yet been willing to do for ourselves.

Perhaps we will become willing to do for our children what we have not yet been willing to do for ourselves

Take a walk through your building and look around. Listen to the conversations that are going on around the water cooler, or over cups of coffee in the local cafeteria. Let yourself overhear the tail end of conversations amongst the support staff as you approach their desks. Stop long enough to notice the faces of the people you walk by on a daily basis. Let yourself look right into their eyes and observe if they look back at you. If so, do their eyes tell the story of participation and contribution or do they betray something else that is going on, deep inside?

Much of the literature available today on organizational change and renewal addresses the structures and the processes and the practices. Although there is much that suggests how we should relate to each other as 'professionals', very little speaks directly to how we could relate to each other as human beings; the experience of being human and being at work. Remember, there's nothing going on at work but individual human beings having conversations with other individual human beings. Very little in the existing literature emphasizes the validity of 'feeling good' about being at work. Historically, it's not mattered much whether or not you felt good about being at work as long as you showed up and did what you were paid

There's nothing going on at work but individual human beings having conversations with other individual human beings to do. Now we know that when people 'feel good' they are more aware, more motivated, more productive and more willing to participate in and fully engage life in general. Sounds like something we'd want to have as part of the work experience.

In many work places today, stress continues to be prevalent. In addition to carrying their briefcases and lunch bags, people are also carrying a lot of anger, resentment and fear. We continue to use demands for more money as the flag we wave to let the powers-that-be know that we are not pleased. And even when the money comes, soon thereafter we are looking for more. It's never enough because that's not what we're mad about.

We continue to use demands for more money to let the powers-that-be know that we are not pleased

Let yourself become aware of the degree to which drugs are present. You would be shocked to know how many of the people you sit next to are taking drugs – prescription and otherwise – to make it possible for them to get through their day. Notice how many people consume liquid lunches or keep bottles of alcohol in their desks or cabinets for 'guests'.

> There was a time, in the early '90's, when we were obsessed with the notion of addiction. You couldn't turn on the T.V. without having Phil or Sally or Oprah discussing yet one more addiction, be it drugs, booze, sex, food, gambling, shopping, exercise – you name it. The bookshelves were stuffed to spilling onto the floor with yet one more piece on how to recover from dysfunctional families, grow your inner child, confront your adult child or let go of your codependency. Have you noticed that today we don't talk about it much anymore? Don't you find it curious that something that captivated us for so long could just disappear like that?

We've replaced that conversation with the one about depression. Have you noticed how depression is now the 'flavor of the week' with books and TV/ radio talk shows directing much attention to this topic? Like addiction, depression comes in its own variety of sub-categories, i.e. bi-polar, clinical. It's also interesting to note that those who carry the label of 'depression' also frequently have or have had issues with alcohol or other substances.

Notice what's happening to corporate Employee Assistance Programs (EAP) costs. Costs are going up as people find it harder and harder to cope from one day to the next. The good news is, at least they're asking for help rather than just slipping away into the deep end of the pool.

Notice all the empty chairs. People who just don't show up anymore; the ones who call in sick regularly for their 'mental health days' or who can't make it in to work today because they just can't face it. Notice the dollar costs associated with hiring temporary staff, or the emotional costs associated with passing off one person's work onto another because they're not here – again. Notice the ones who are physically there and could care less. The empty eyes say it all. They show up on a regular basis to ensure that the paycheck keeps coming and they have no interest at all in what they're doing. Many of the more adventurous ones may actually be running their own businesses from their office, using the company phones/faxes/computers to do something that they really care about.

All in all, work places are not fun places to be

All in all, work places are not fun places to be. But then, what are we to expect from places where it's okay to bring your intellect but in poor taste not to leave the rest of you at home? What are we to expect from places that welcome what we have to give and are ill-equipped to give back anything beyond the dollars that we hold to be valuable? The days drag on and the rewards are minimal. There comes a point where even the paycheck isn't enough. From time to time, we find ourselves genuinely engaged in doing something interesting, something that invites us to grow or stretch or experience something new. But most of the time, it's the same old thing, from one day to the next. How did we get to this state?

Think about work as water and the people who go there as the fish. We spend much of our time focused on the fish. We talk about good fish, bad fish; right fish, wrong fish; fish with attitude problems and fish in personality conflicts with the boss fish. We're sure that if we could just get the right fish in the right job, get the fish trained or get certain fish to go away – maybe retire early – then everything would work out. What we often fail to notice (because we can't see what we're not looking for) is that the water that the fish are swimming in is polluted. No matter how robust and magnificent your fish, it's just a matter of time before all the fish need a little boost or some kind of external supplement to keep them moving. But no matter what you do, they will eventually lose vitality – and maybe even their lives – if they continue to live in polluted water. It would help if we began to pay attention to the fact that the water is polluted.

In our work environments, the water is the behavioral environment that we, the fish, operate in. In my more than 25 years of life in organizational systems, rarely have I come across people who have been dissatisfied with the actual task of the work that they were doing. Their greatest difficulty and complaints came from the environment in which they were doing the task: the dishonesty, the withheld information, the back-stabbing, the gossip, the complaining and the bickering. These are the things that make life intolerable for us in these environments. The behavioral context within

The behavioral context within which we operate has a profound effect on our physical, emotional and spiritual well-being which we operate has a profound effect on our physical, emotional and spiritual well-being. And we are the ones who have polluted the water.

Notice the way people interact at work. How often do you get the sense that there is something else going on that you don't know about? How do you feel about the gossiping; and the whining and the complaining; and the back-stabbing? How often do you participate in it? How often do you feel that you are being told the truth? Honesty is an interesting thing. We hear from others – and say ourselves – that all we want is to be told the truth. Yet, how often do we tell the truth ourselves? How frequently do we take that first step to reveal rather than hang back and wait for something to be revealed to us? How often are we a part of the problem?

The difficulties that we are experiencing at work are a microcosm of what we are experiencing generally at all levels of the culture. It's in the boardroom and it's in our living rooms

The difficulties that we are experiencing at work are a microcosm of what we are experiencing generally at all levels of the culture. It's in the boardroom and it's in our living rooms. It's in our schools and our churches and our day-care centers. It has spilled over into every area of our life because everywhere we go, there we are. It's not just about work - it's about us wherever we happen to be.

Given how much of our life is spent at work and given that work is an experience that we will all, at some point in the unfolding of our lives, have in common that we can all understand and relate to, it makes sense that we would focus so much of our attention on it. It's also safe as a context for the discussion, since we consider it to be 'public' and therefore, neutral.

We have been drawn to focus our attention on the problem and how it manifests at work because it's safe. That's the one place where we can approach a problem from a public, professional, objective, detached, impersonal way. We keep the problem at arm's length and not too close to home. It is also legitimized since we are being paid by someone else and who are we to question the validity of such an inquiry? So, if they decide to rework the system, how can we argue? The problem is that, as big as the 'work' system is, the problem has even overgrown that system!

We continue to create work environments that are structured according to the parent-child model. It makes perfect sense for us to do that since that is what we know best. We build organizational systems (or educational systems, health systems, church systems, medical systems, etc.) that are larger organic living systems (more on this later) that reflect its creators.

We continue to create work environments that are structured according to the parent-child model

We have made work a place where the boss (mom or dad, but usually dad) is in charge and the employees (kids) aren't. We have created systems where a few (the boss/parents) are in charge of the many (the employees/kids). We have developed contexts for work that are crazy-making, telling us to do one thing (we want you to tell us the truth) while clearly unable to tolerate the result (shoot the messenger). Like children, we will only reveal to the parents what we believe they are capable of hearing and can tolerate. And also like children, when the kids rebel (create unions and start talking back), the parents feel oppressed and unfairly treated. After all, they say, they are doing their best.

Some of the characteristics that have become very common in the work / life are listed in *Figure* 2. Let yourself browse through them and remember to breathe as you go through. Also notice when you catch yourself holding your breath. That's a clue that you're onto a good one! This list is not necessarily complete, so feel free to add your personal favorites.

Sometimes, it's difficult for people to stay focused on these characteristics, one of the reasons being that they don't just surface at work. These are also common to the structures of our family systems, striking too close to

BEHAVIOURAL CHARACTERISTICS

DENIAL DISHONESTY SCARCITY
DEFENSIVENESS PERFECTIONISM
ILLUSION OF CONTROL SELF-CENTREDNESS
CRISIS ORIENTATION CONFUSION
GRANDIOSITY BLAME GUILT DISTRUST
FEAR SHAME RIGIDITY
ISOLATION LOSS OF HUMOR RESENTMENT
ETHICAL DETERIORATION

THINKING PROCESSES

OVERLY LOGICAL AND RATIONAL
COMPULSIVE DUALISTIC
MEMORY LOSS / BLACKOUTS

Figure 2: Work / Life Environments

home to allow us to focus on them for any length of time without experiencing a familiar discomfort. Often, when working with people who are in positions of leadership or management or leverage in their organization, there is a great desire to quickly move past these 'negative' traits and move forward into something positive; to get on with it and to stop dwelling on the 'negative'. The difficulty with this response is that quickly moving on does not make them disappear. If anything, moving quickly into seeking a solution perpetuates our on-going fear of these traits, leaving us at their mercy. And yet, all we are running from is ourselves.

It is important to note that in today's world most behavioural environments are closed loop systems (see Figure 3) and can include families, individuals, work, social organizations of church, school, community groups, etc.

We cannot change these systems with the very same behaviors that created them. In order to change these systems, we must be able to *participate in* them without *being driven by* them. We must be able to be *in them* yet not be *of them*. We must also own these behaviors in ourselves so that we do not fear them in others. Then, and only then, do we have what it takes to let them go and do something else instead. Once they no longer drive us, we can even begin to find humor when we come face-to-face with them.

We cannot change these systems with the very same behaviors that created these systems

Open loop and Closed loop Systems

Collectively, these form the behavioral characteristics of a closed loop system (*Figure 3*). What's inside the circle stays in the circle: nothing leaves and nothing new can get in. It is like hermetically sealing our fate. The information/people/practices/world-views already inside the circle keep going round and round, perhaps shifting position from time to time (like the deck chairs on the Titanic!), but nothing unfamiliar takes place.

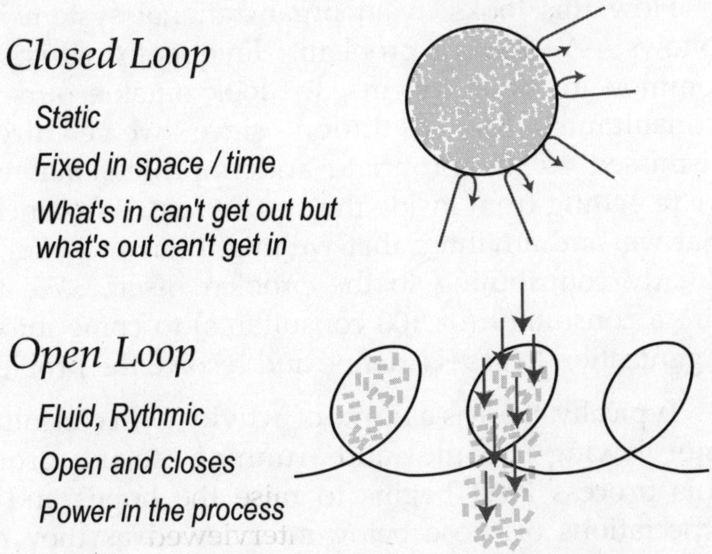

Figure 3: Open and Closed Loop Systems

If you are attempting to penetrate a closed-loop system, your observations of the status quo or suggestions for change will be met with statements like: we can't do that – we've never done it before; or, we did that five years ago and it didn't work; or, we can't do that, the boss/president/parent/leader/manager won't approve – even though the boss/president/parent/leader/manager never even gets a chance to consider it directly. The result of this guarded position is that what's inside the loop stays inside the loop and nothing new gets in.

The structure is static: without movement and feeding off itself

The structure is static: without movement and feeding off itself. You can imagine that over time, the health of this system would become questionable. But because we instinctively know that movement is a sign of life, we have an on-going need to take some kind of action. And yet in a closed-loop system, any movement is inside the loop itself – like a rat in a cage. 'Round and 'round it goes, often frantically speeding itself up to allow for a sense of purposefulness, trying to reach… somewhere. But nothing really changes.

How this looks in an organizational system is as follows. We have a problem. Frequently, as is quite common in these systems, we look outside ourselves (consultants) for resolution since we've already dismissed as inappropriate and unprofessional what we're getting from inside the system (us). We conclude that we, and anything that we might have to offer, are already contributing to the problem itself. We then hire a consultant (or 100 consultants) to come into the organization to assess, define and resolve the problem.

Typically, there is a flurry of activity with consultants interviewing people and running focus groups. This process itself begins to raise the hopes and the expectations of those being interviewed as they now believe that someone is actually listening to them and that something is going to be different. Anticipation builds as people wait, holding their breath, to witness the marvel of the results.

Interviews and analysis complete, the consultant(s) conclude that the problem is, say, span of control (a frequent favorite!). Now, the flurry of activity is in the Human Resources/Personnel Division as org charts are redesigned, new job descriptions are created and people are moved around. Several months go by, the dust finally settles and people begin to notice that although things are different, nothing has really changed. The same old problems are still there.

Although things are different, nothing has really changed

Recognizing we've hired the 'wrong' consultants, we begin looking for the 'right' consultant. Approximately 18 months go by, when the next round of experts arrive at our place of work. And we do it again. Only this time, it's not news. This time, when we're being interviewed and 'focused' on, we're a little more jaded than we were the last time, maybe slightly less forth coming and beginning to lean to the skeptical side of things. Once again, time goes by, the interviews and the analysis are complete and we now conclude that our problem is… technology!

Again, a great flurry of activity (not to mention strain on the budget) as new technology (hardware and software and its accompanying challenges) makes its way onto every desk in the organization. People grumble through being trained on software they'll likely never click on once the fuss is over and done with. And once again, several months go by, the dust finally settles and we begin to notice that although things are different, nothing's really changed. Only now, we've moved from skeptical to cynical. The trail home is getting steeper and longer.

The alternative is an open-loop system. Simply put, its major distinguishing factor is that not only does it allow for movement, it expects it as a natural state. Movement is a sign of life! An open-loop system also allows for space since without space, movement is not possible. As the movement occurs, it expands into the unknown around it – rather than circling inside itself – taking up unknown territory. The movement that it invites is at the level of the larger system, driven by the movement of the smaller, individual systems that are contained in the larger system.

You'll notice that an open-loop system starts out like a closed-loop one: a closed circle. But at some point in time, it becomes evident from some kind of pain response that something isn't working. Rather than trying to stop the pain inside the loop by silencing it (like taking drugs), there is a recognition that the pain is a communication of something… that it is a legitimate message about and a symptom of something else. A conscious choice is engaged and a decision is made to open the loop and to move into the pain; to engage what's causing it, to move toward it rather than away from it and to engage it directly ourselves – rather than to distance ourselves by bringing into the system experts from the outside – since the system is nothing more than a reflection of who we are.

Outside experts will not know what to do with our pain since they will have had no experience of its formation and the secrets that hold it in place

Who knows better than we do what is going on inside of us? As well-intentioned as they may be, outside experts will not know what to do with our pain since they will have had no experience of its formation and the secrets that hold it in place.

How we open the loop is by acknowledging that something isn't working and we open ourselves to new information. Perhaps a course or a book or a set of CD's. More importantly, perhaps a conversation – finally engaging in that conversation that we've been avoiding for some time now – perhaps talking to the people inside the system that irritate us the most. The loop opens long enough for new information, new experiences and new insights to wash over the system, some of it deemed to be relevant and some of it passing through. In addition, some of the old begins to fall away as well, moving out of the system. Eventually, the system closes once again to restabilize – only this time, it will have done so at a higher order, having restructured the old with the new, creating something entirely different.

The power of the open-loop system is in the process itself. There is a rhythm of opening and closing; entering and leaving; unfolding and enfolding; expanding and collapsing. Somewhat like the natural rhythms of the planet, like the sun coming up and going down; or the tides coming in and going out; or your own breath, inhaling and exhaling. Without these rhythms, we could not survive. Were you to inhale and hold your breath forever, or exhale and hold your breath forever, you'd die. What makes us think that the systems we create, the systems that are a reflection of us and of which we are an integral part, could function in any other way?

The power of the open-loop system is in the process itself

A closed-loop system will have behavioral characteristics that will be grounded in a context of fear: fear of loss, fear of pain, fear of the unknown, fear of failure, fear of falling off the edge of the world. An open-loop system is grounded in a context of trust: trust of self, trust that we can handle it, trust that not only will we succeed but we'll have fun in the process, trust that the world is round. How would you prefer to live?

A closed-loop system is grounded in a context of fear

An open-loop system is grounded in a context of trust

In the next chapter, we'll look at how we got to be like this; how we learned that the world is flat; and how we came to be so frightened of not having control. Remember, I don't believe that we are broken or puny or dysfunctional. We have become who we are for very good reasons and with the best of intentions. The problem is that it no longer serves us given where we want to go, who we want to become and what we want out of life.

Since there's nothing going on in our work/life but individual human beings interacting with other individual human beings, it becomes very important to better understand who we are as individual human beings – not resources or groups or teams or a mass of humanity but as singular and unique expressions of life. Having a greater awareness of and respect for ourselves as individuals makes it possible for us to better understand and respect each other. You can't give what you haven't got!

Having a greater awareness of and respect for ourselves as individuals makes it possible for us to better understand and respect each other

I think we've spent more than enough time on the fact that work environments (amongst others) aren't working very well. That's not news. It's time for us to find another way to define 'the problem', at a higher level of thinking. The alternative is to keep doing the same thing, over and over again, expecting to achieve a different result. We already know that's the definition of insanity.

For more information, consider:

- *The Addictive Organization* by Anne Wilson-Schaef and Diane Fassel
- *Leadership and the New Science* by Margaret Wheatley
- *The Turning Point: Science, Society and the Rising Culture* by Fritjof Capra
- *Pathways to Personal Power* by Louise LeBrun

FULLY ALIVE

You have brains in your head.
You have feet in your shoes.
You can steer yourself
Any direction you choose.
You're on your own.
And you know what you know.
And you are the one
Who'll decide where to go.

- Dr. Seuss -

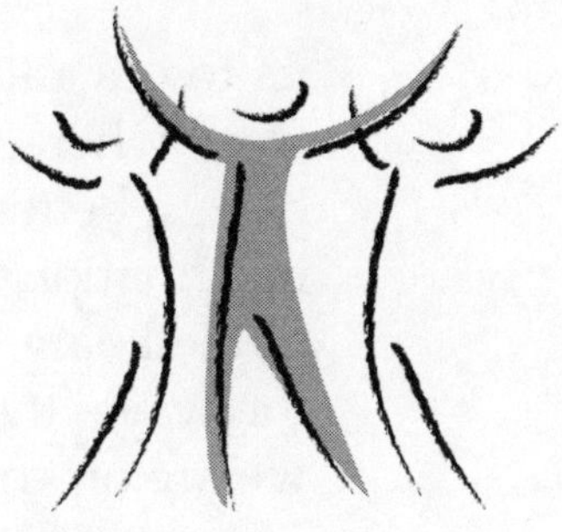

CHAPTER 4

Claiming It

How did this happen?

It is not by accident that we have created our work, family and educational systems to be what they are. But nor is it necessarily by design! Much of what we have today is simply a matter of inheritance as it has been for the generation before that, and the one before that. It would seem to be reasonable that if we do not like what we have, all we have to do is change it. Do something else. That may sound simple and yet may not be quite as easy as we'd like it to be.

It is a fine and noble thing to focus on the future and on creating something good for all humankind. However, what I have had to learn the hard way is that if I try to ignore the obvious and turn my back on it with the hope that if I can't see it, it won't be there, it will sink its mighty teeth into my back and never let go. It's tough to move into the future with commitment, vitality and joy when the truth of my day-to-day experience has dug in its heels – relentlessly – and refuses to surrender and disappear.

How will I ever know what's missing if I have no idea of what I already have? In order for us to get where we want to go (that is, assuming we have any idea where that is), we first have to know where we are so that we can set off in a direction that will take us to our ultimate destination. Before we can move on from where we are, from what we have now, we must have a better understanding of how we got here. This information will allow us to avoid the pitfalls of the past while being better able to respond to the signals along the way – the road markers – that tell us whether or not we are on course. With that information, we can adjust as we go, just like that jet that takes you off to your holiday in the sun.

Our work, family and educational systems are our own creations. And sometimes good intentions are not enough. It would seem that like Dr. Frankenstein, although we set out to create something good, we may have created our own version of what has become, for many of us, a monster. Maybe it's time to go back to the drawing board.

How did we get to be who we are?

Since work is a larger organic living system that is driven by the smaller, individual organic living systems that are its fundamental components, it becomes crucial to better understand the structure of an individual living system and how these come together to create the larger living systems of family, community or work.

Figure 4 says it all in one snapshot. Let's explore what it means in some detail.

If I were to stand before you, I would look like one thing to you that you would call 'Louise'. And yet, we now know from science that I am not one thing but a collection of a multitude of living things, each interacting with the other. Inside me there is a collection of living systems, such as a digestive system, a circulatory system, an endocrine system, a respiratory system, and a nervous system, to name a few. The degree to which I will experience well-being is the degree to which each of these systems, in and of itself, is fully functional and the degree to which these systems interact in a healthy, life-sustaining way. If we were to dive into any one particular system, we would soon discover that it, too, is comprised of other living systems (organs, tissue, cells, etc.) all interacting with the same underlying principle for well-being. However, let's move our attention out and into creating a larger system than the one I am as an individual.

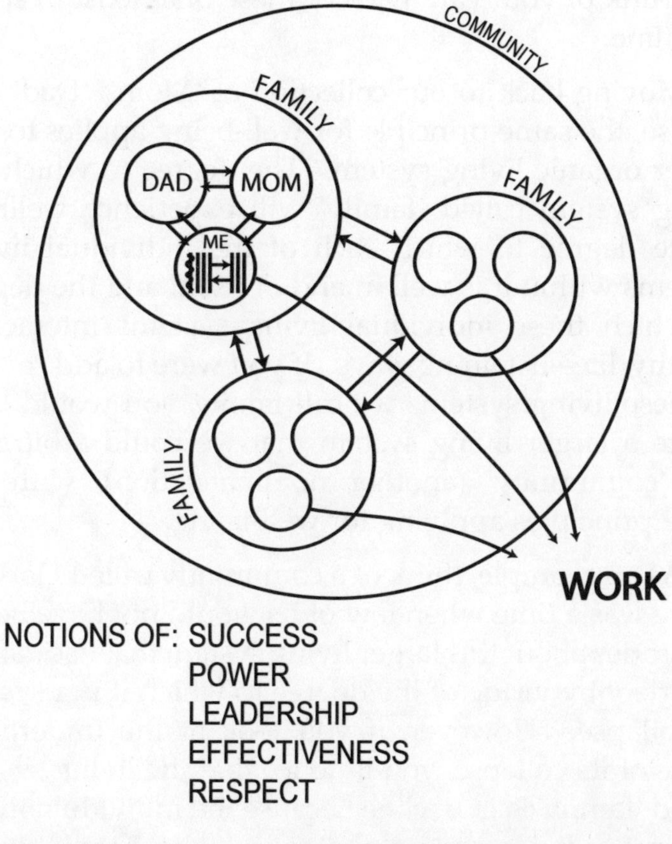

Figure 4: Nested Living Systems™

If you were to add another individual living system called 'Dad' and another individual living system called 'Mom', you would now create a larger living system called 'family'. Here's something important to note: the word 'family' is what's called a *nominalization*. We have taken something that is a living, moving, changing expression of an experience and turned it into a noun. We have taken something that is constantly shifting and have tried to make it static – make it stand still. You cannot put a pound of 'family' in the trunk of your car like you can with other nouns, like table or trout. The word 'family' represents a notion or a concept; it is short hand for something that represents certain things to us. You can however, put either Mom or Dad or Louise in the trunk of your car. Each of these does exist in space and time.

Moving back to our collection of 'Mom', 'Dad' and Louise, the same principle for well-being applies to this larger organic living system. The degree to which the living system called 'family' will experience wellness is the degree to which each of the individual living systems within it is well in and of itself, and the degree to which these individual living systems interact in healthy, life-sustaining ways. If you were to add several of these living systems we call family, you would then create a larger living system that we could arbitrarily call 'community' (another nominalization), with the same principles applying for well-being.

As an example, think of a community called Harlem. There was a time when few of us would not have heard the stories about this larger living system that has gained notoriety by virtue of the degree to which it is a system in collapse. However, if you look at the underlying cause of its collapse, you'll notice that the living system called 'family' is in decline because the individual living systems called 'mom' or 'dad' are no longer individually well or interacting in healthy, life-sustaining ways. The fundamental operating unit in any living system is always the individual.

The fundamental operating unit in any living system is always the individual

You can continue to move outward and you'll have communities coming together to form larger living systems called cities; cities coming together to form larger living systems called states or provinces; states or provinces forming countries; countries forming continents; continents forming planets, planets forming solar systems; etc. In the structuring of the systems from which we live, we are the creators of those experiences and affect much larger systems (eco-systems of the planet) by the choices we make. It is not by accident – nor necessarily by conscious design – that we are who we've become.

It is not by accident – nor necessarily by conscious design – that we are who we've become

We spend more waking time at work than anywhere else in our adult lives. So, who exactly is it that's going to work? You come out of your family system, I come out of mine and Joe down the hall comes out of his and we all go to work, bringing with us the structure of our 'reality'. We don't ever talk about any of this experience because it's personal. Work isn't a place to talk about such things, since we're supposed to focus on the job, keep it professional, and get on with it.

The trouble is that each of us is shaped by those very family systems – by the beliefs, values and attitudes of that system – that come to work with us. That information is wired right into the nervous system in the body – and try going to work without your body! To suggest that we should leave this out of the equation is to suggest that our intellects can survive without the rest of us. And yet, even though we know today that our belief systems are the actual structures of and perceptual filters for our experience, there's no room for us to discuss these in the work place. Does that make sense to you?

Team work!

Let's say that you and I are part of a team. Our job is to come together to get something done. We are willing to talk about the team succeeding and accomplishing and getting the job done, and how we're going to go about getting that done. But the one conversation we rarely have is: what does success mean? The word 'success' is a nominalization – you can't put a pound of success in the trunk of your car. Nominalizations are words that represent things and yet we never explore with each other what this particular word represents for each of us on the team. We just assume it means the same thing to everyone. Maybe – but maybe not!

What if we were to talk about it? If you were to ask me what 'success' means to me, you might want to know, "How would you know when you've been successful?" My answer could be that I'd know I had been successful when I had a 5000 square foot house on the Nepali Coast in Kauai (with staff, of course), a fire red Jaguar sitting in the driveway, a yacht with crew, all the money I'd ever want and I'd only work when I felt like it.

Someone may ask you the same question. Perhaps your answer would be you'd know you'd been successful when your children grew up and came home to spend time with you, not because it was Christmas and they felt obligated but because they really like being around you.

Two very different world views. The first is driven by acquisitions; the second is driven by relationships. The former is externally based; the latter is internally based. For me, I would be willing to sacrifice the quality of relationships to 'get the job done'. For you, you would be willing to compromise the task in order to maintain the quality of the relationships. We may well end up having difficulty working together, feeling sabotaged, hard done by or that there are hidden agendas. We end up blaming, judging and resenting each other because we never, ever talk about it. That's personal and there's no place for that at work. I wonder how often the difficulties we have at work could be resolved with a simple conversation about ourselves?

We end up blaming, judging and resenting each other because we never, ever talk about it. That's personal and there's no place for that at work

The great leveler

Given that there is nothing going on at work but individual human beings interacting with other individual human beings; and given that the individual human being is the fundamental operating unit in any living system, it becomes crucial to better understand how we, as individuals, are shaped and molded. For this reason, we'll explore the Androgynous Baby™ in *Figure 5*.

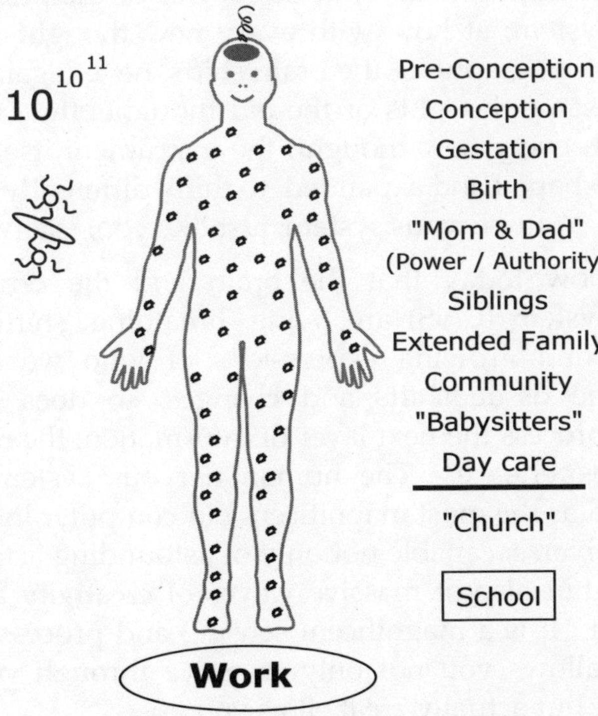

Figure 5: Androgynous Baby™

There are certain things around the world that are common to the experience of being human. Before you are your gender, or the color of your skin, or your particular religious affiliation or your education, you are first and foremost human. That fundamental truth goes with you wherever you go. And there are certain very predictable experiences that are common to every human being, no matter where you came from.

The first of these is that we arrive with the basic design being one of a number of organs, structures and systems in a 'bag' called the body, including a brain and a nervous system. We have learned more about the brain and the nervous system in the last 10 years than we had known in the previous 100. This is not rocket science. You need read only the more popularized journals, like *Discover* or *MacLean's* or *Time* magazine, to find articles that marvel at the power of the human nervous system; at how with every new thought you think, the topography of the brain shifts, never again to think the same thoughts or the old thoughts the same way. With every new thought, the instrument itself is literally reshaped and expanded, to think differently the next time. Your nervous system, just like you, is alive.

Your nervous system, just like you, is alive

We know today that the brain and the central nervous system (CNS) are living, breathing, shifting, changing and growing expressions of who we are; that as the tissue shifts and changes, so does our ability to process the next layer of information; the next layer of experience. The human nervous system is recognized as the most magnificent bio-computer in the known universe, capable not only of astounding acts of repetition but also of massive waves of creativity and innovation. It is a magnificent sensing and processing unit that allows you not only to move through your experience but actually create it as you go.

We all have a brain and a nervous system. As we come to better understand it and make friends with it, our capacity to fully express and create causes the world to be permanently altered. Here's what a couple of people have to say about you as a bio-processor.

Dr. Bruce Lipton, Ph.D., (Cellular Biologist) from *The Biology of Consciousness:*

"A brain comprised of two cells would function exactly like the "brain" in any single cell, only it would express significantly more information processing capacity. Likewise, a brain of five cells would process information, or "*think*", in the same manner as a single cell however, it would express vastly more awareness. A human brain of 500 billion cells (neurons and glia) processes information, or *thinks*, using the same mechanisms employed by a single cell. However, the collective unquantifiable awareness capacity of our massive information system provides enough memory and processing power to express the quality of self-consciousness, the basis of *mind* and the foundation of human consciousness."

Did you know how enormously powerful you already are, let alone your potential for becoming? Read on:

Dr. Paul Goodwin, from '*Foundation Theory*':

"*The Complexity*: Assuming that the fully developed human brain contains on the order of 100 billion neurons and that virtually no new neurons are added after birth, it can be calculated that neurons must be generated in the developing brain at an average rate of more than 250,000 per minute. Additionally, assuming each neuron will ultimately connect to between 1,000 and 100,000 others, and that at birth the human brain possesses about 70% of its mature connections, it can be calculated that the 'wires' connecting one neuron with another in the developing fetus must be put into place at a rate exceeding 175 million per minute, or some 3 million per second. It is estimated that the mature human brain contains approximately 100 trillion neural wires.

(Children grow) about 15 trillion neural wires during their first six formative years… an average of about 2.5 trillion wires a year. This translates to 6.8 billion wires per day, or 280 million per hour, or 4.7 million wires (synapses) per minute!"

Perhaps you can better understand and appreciate the incredible damage potential of ingesting chemicals during pregnancy. The effects on the developing fetus are profound. And finally:

Dr. Deepak Chopra, taken from one of his many awe-inspiring books, *Quantum Healing*:

"If you could see your body as it really is, you would never see it the same way twice. Ninety-eight percent of the atoms in your body were not there a year ago. The skeleton that seems so solid was not there three months ago. The configuration of the bone cells remains somewhat constant, but atoms of all kinds pass freely back and forth through the cell walls, and by that means you acquire a new skeleton every three months.

The skin is new every month. You have a new stomach lining every four days, with the actual surface cells that contact food being renewed every five minutes. The cells in the liver turn over very slowly but new atoms still flow through them, like water in a river course, making a new liver every six weeks. Even within the brain, whose cells are not replaced once they die, the content of carbon, nitrogen, oxygen, and so on it totally different today from a year ago."

We are only now beginning to understand the incredible potential of who we are as human beings; and of the enormous potential that we *are* for expression.

We have known from science for sometime now that the average human being thinks about 65,000 thoughts a day. That's the good news; the bad news is that more than 90% of these thoughts are exactly the same as the ones we thought yesterday! (Small wonder life feels repetitive.) There was also a time when we believed that we only used about 10% of brain capability, meaning that we were only accessing 10% of our own potential. What we now know today is that it's not 10% but closer to 2% - and that includes the part of the CNS that runs the body. Imagine what life could be like if we went from 2% to 3%…

Your nervous system manages about 3 trillion cellular interactions per minute, creates a new stomach lining for you every four days and completely rebuilds your skeletal structure every nine months. What have you done for it lately? It also keeps your heart beating, digests your lunch, keeps air moving in and out of your lungs and flows the blood through your veins. And it does all this, and much more, even while you sleep.

Another thing your nervous system does for you is that it allows you to develop habits so that you don't have to 'figure it out' each and every time. Think of driving a standard shift, for example. The first time you get into the car, and start doing all those things at the same time... well, let's put it this way... first gear's a bummer! But very quickly, your body learns how to drive so that you can focus your attention on other things (like playing with the radio dial, or talking on the phone, or lighting a cigarette). Your body very quickly takes the information required for the mechanics of driving and creates a pattern of response. Before you know it, driving is a breeze – effortless! - even to the point where you often drive home in such an automaton state that you miss your highway exit!

That your body creates these kinds of habits can be quite useful. However, it will also create habituated responses to people and situations. In other words, you'll develop automatic responses to people, places and things, with an automated response being one that just kicks in without any aware thought on your part. Habituated responses are mindless; they take place in the body. The quality of your life may be served in some ways by these habituated responses (like driving a standard shift) and may not necessarily be served by such a response in other areas (such as your interactions with your spouse, your children, and your boss). It may be useful to become more familiar with what habits are already installed and where they came from.

Habituated responses are mindless; they take place in the body

In addition to the basic physical aspects, there are also a number of processes that we are all exposed to that are wired directly into the CNS. Remember that your nervous system never sleeps, so even while you do, your nervous system (or body) is very busy logging everything away for future reference. Nothing is too small to be overlooked. And, given that we are bombarded with about 2 billion bits of information per minute, it's quite a job.

The inevitable and the unavoidable

The first process that we are all exposed to is the process of gestation. Give or take a couple of weeks, it takes us about nine months to get here. There is a very precise, predictable sequence that we follow as we travel down the path to humanoid and the birth experience. That comes next and as far as I know there are still only two ways to get here: vaginal delivery and Caesarian section. None of us is hatched! And we know from hypnosis that many people can recall the actual birth process with memories that are validated by the people who were around them at the time. The information is there to be retrieved.

Next comes our experience of what we call 'mom and dad', or our first encounter with what we will come to know as power and authority. The words are in quotes because it could mean biological parent(s), foster parents, an older sibling, the nice lady next door or your babysitter. The structure of the experience is less important than the presence of the experience itself. These first early experiences will set the stage for the way you come to respond to authority and power – and the people who represent them – in later years.

Each of us carries, deep inside of us, information that is unique to our structuring of the world in which we live. These experiences, from conception through to our death, are wired directly into the nervous system and literally shape who we become. Traditional psychologists believe that our core beliefs – meaning our beliefs about ourselves (good person, bad person); our beliefs about the world (safe, unsafe) and our beliefs about our ability to manage in our world (competent, incompetent) are in place by the time we are five years old. Personally, having had two children and having worked with adults now for close to 20 years, I believe they are in place much earlier.

Each of us carries, deep inside of us, information that is unique to our structuring of the world in which we live

For most of us, we rarely if ever revisit those core beliefs as structured and defined through the experiences of a five year old. Just ask yourself: when was the last time you thought about what you believe, about what really matters to you – not what someone else wants you to believe, or thinks you should believe, but what really matters to you? If it's been a while, you also have to ask yourself: who's driving the bus?

When was the last time you thought about what you believe, about what really matters to you – not what someone else wants you to believe, or thinks you should believe, but what really matters to you?

Is it any surprise that we become 'adults' and, when certain circumstances present themselves, we feel like children? Have you ever noticed that you're an intelligent, articulate, capable and responsible human being until you visit your mother and then, all of a sudden, you're eight? What is it that is stored inside of us that leaves us believing in our own powerlessness, helplessness and dependence? The information from our experiences during these early years does not disappear; it becomes part of that miraculous living system that we are and creates the platform on which we stand when we move into our future. How many of us have any idea what's going on in there?

Add to this already potent mix experiences with siblings; extended family, church/Sunday school; babysitters and daycare; Brownies, Cubs, T-Ball and choir practice and all the people and adventures we have; and finally, what I refer to fondly as 'Boot Camp for life' – school – and you can imagine what we carry around with us. In addition, many of these experiences are in place before we have language, wired directly into the nervous system without the benefit of the buffer of language. It all adds up to quite a trip. Then we all grow up, go to work and expect work to work without ever paying attention to how we got to be the person who shows up from 9 to 5. The next time you're in a meeting, look around the table. None of us has been spared this predictable journey into adulthood.

Most of us don't have a clue who we are

Most of us don't have a clue who we are. We don't have a clue what's wired into our early experience. If you, like me, were born more than twenty years ago, mainstream thinking would have taught you that it didn't matter what was deep inside and unique to you; that what matters is what's in your head or your intellect, what's going on since you've 'arrived' or become able to have an intelligent conversation with an adult. We now know that's not true. Not only is it not true - it's often deadly to continue to ignore it.

We also now know that although we've been trained to operate from what is referred to as linguistically structured thought – meaning that how we think the process of thinking occurs is in words and phrases – there is much more occurring inside the body. We have now become aware of the surface structure and the deep structure of language.

For thousands of years, ancient wisdom has proffered the notion of energy centers in the body, or chakras, that are like generators that keep the body energy, or life force, moving freely. Many trained in the traditional allopathic world view have, up until recently, dismissed this notion as ludicrous, as there was no 'evidence' that could be measured either with the naked eye or with existing instrumentation. However, with the existence of Kirlian photography and with the more recent discoveries of scientists such as Dr. Candace Pert (*Molecules of Emotion*) or Dr. Valerie Hunt (*Infinite Mind: The Vibrations of Human Consciousness*), we are becoming more aware of the power of the human body and the implication of the presence of an electromagnetic field that surrounds the body and all living things.

There is a correlation between the movement of energy through the electromagnetic field, the process of thought as we have come to know it, the movement of energy and information through bio-chemical and electrochemical impulses through the body and our sense of personal power. Given that few of us were taught any of this in Grade 10 biology/science classes or even beyond at the University level, how well do we know how to decode the messages of the body and their relationship to our thought?

Home-grown strategies for living

Our families of origin are the context within which we learn to shape our identity

Our families of origin are the context within which we learn to shape our identity. They are the molds into which we are poured and the intense heat within which we are fired and glazed into who we ultimately become. Our identities (our way of defining us to ourselves and to others; our ability to give ourselves permission to do and not do; our capacity to applaud and forgive ourselves and others; our beliefs about ourselves, our world and our effectiveness in moving through that world) are designed and dictated by our families of origin. We learn to 'know our place' and to replicate what 'we always/never do/don't do that in this family' without question and without hope of it ever being otherwise.

For many of us, even as mature, responsible adults, we have no idea what is genuinely meaningful to us. We know only what is expected of us and what we are responsible for.

Over the years, I've discovered that one of the most powerful ways to explore this part of our evolution is in the language of family system's roles. You may be familiar with these, having been given names like Family Hero, Lost Child, Scapegoat and Mascot. In the existing literature on recovery from addiction, as well as in the works of Virginia Satir (pioneer in family systems therapy) and others, these roles will exist in some form or other.

This conversation about family systems, roles and strategies is a huge one! When we dive into the deep end of this pool, it takes five to seven days to move through and is preceded by in excess of 200 hours of preparation. (I learned a long time ago and the hard way (of course!) that without new information, we are destined to have the conversation the same way, over and over again. That new information is essential to our being able to move beyond the confines of the box we find ourselves in with regard to family. And not just any box but one that is padlocked and bound for safekeeping!) Nonetheless, to ensure that you have at least an overview, here's the short version.

A family is not a 'thing' – it's an experience. It is not lifeless and static but is a living, breathing, moving, changing, sentient expression of the living, organic beings who come together for a shared purpose. Without those people, 'family' would cease to exist. 'Family' is a label that we affix to that collective experience, using the word as a form of short-hand or code word for that experience.

A family is not a 'thing' – it's an experience

Family systems are living organic systems and are as alive and vibrant and expansive and life-sustaining as the people who create them and comprise them. Families and the people in them are the way that we replicate ourselves in organized, 'civilized' society; passing down, from one generation to the next, how we're supposed to behave, what we're supposed to care about and the standards by which we measure ourselves and each other as good/bad, right/wrong, etc. Growing up in our families is how we discover who we are, who we might become and what we can/can't give ourselves permission to do/be.

Families and the people in them are the way that we replicate ourselves in organized

Families and the people in them are the way we create fractals (or subsets of the primary set of origin) for the creation of our larger social structures that make up our civilization. Like a head of cauliflower is formed by the coming together of the smaller flowerets, so the flowerets reflect the overall pattern of the whole cauliflower, each a replication of the other. We see it in our children; in how we and our children come together as a collective called 'family' with each of the children being a replica of the parents that come before. Children do what we do and become who we are in the world. Children are fractals of their parents. Our families are the cookie cutters for creating larger and larger collectives of human beings, and bigger and bigger supplies of labor for the larger collective. Without mindfulness, our lives repeat the patterns of these family systems, or the flip side. However, individuality demands that we awaken to the mindful choice.

In the last 60 years, work by people like Virginia Satir and others, as well as research in the field of addiction, co-dependence and family systems relationships, has offered us new perspectives on what families are, how they work and what's important for us to pay attention to.

'Family' is a nominalization. You can't put a pound of 'family' in the trunk of your car

'Family' is a nominalization. You can't put a pound of 'family' in the trunk of your car. You can only put the individual persons who come together to create the experience of 'family'. Another use of nominalization is in the labels we put to certain predictable clusters of behavior that come together to form what we call 'behavioral profiles' or 'personality types' (all of these words, by the way, are also nominalizations) like: Family Hero, Lost Child, Scapegoat and Mascot.

What we've discovered from working with people for more than 20 years is that Family Hero, Lost Child, etc. are not about personality or character, they are ways of coping with our lives – with our experiences – that are learned in the genius of our desire and ability to function effectively and (in some families) survive. They are reflections of ways that we have discovered how to engage for results that we hold as meaningful and/or relevant in our lives. They are strategies that we engage and become very good at, as we move through space and time. Events and circumstances will trigger a need within us to respond or engage, and each of these labels represents a pattern of response that we most easily turn to in order for us to make sense of our world.

Following is a very brief overview of the collection of behaviors identified for each of these roles. The emotion identified with the characteristic of section indicates the primary internal state that each of these roles is intended to mask, minimize or overcome.

Family Hero: The responsible one; 'The Fixer'; overachiever; does well in school; charming; ease with language, often talks a great deal; quick to learn and do; all-together; perfectionist; demanding of self and others; tireless; relentless; can always do one more thing – are the clydesdales of the work environment. **Signature emotion -** ***shame***

Family Heroes often end up in management jobs; as organizational or community leaders. They are the ones who tend to burn out before they notice their own fatigue levels and drop like a rock!

Lost Child: Isolates; is often experienced as distant and aloof; often 'shy'; quiet; few friends; often feels different; left out; the 'invisible' one in the family. **Signature emotion -** ***sadness***

Lost Children are often working in libraries and in high-tech. They prefer things to people; and like work that they can do on their own.

Scapegoat: Acts out; often the one to abuse substances; hates authority (parents, teachers, coaches, etc.); often in trouble with the law; takes unnecessary risks; strong peer connection; often sullen/angry; seeks confrontation; quick to blame everyone else; lives life with an 'edge'. **Signature emotion -** ***anger / rage***

Scapegoats are often attracted to work that demands physical strength. They tend to gather in packs ('the boys', gangs, etc.) and prefer to be with their peers.

Clown: Often 'hyper-active'; always moving; being super-cute; will do anything to attract attention; humor often inappropriate; social convener; anything for a laugh; can't understand why someone's feelings are hurt. **Signature emotion** - ***fear / inadequacy***

Clowns seek out opportunities to gather with others, often drawn to support work in the services areas. Their belief is that all problems can be solved if people just get along – and that demands an office party or BBQ!

As you read through these lists, you may identify more strongly with one set over another. You may also find that you relate to one group as dominant, with those of another group also calling to you. In truth, typically, we develop comfort with a variety of responses over time, frequently shifting from one to another as our situations change, our goals change and our ability to separate from our family of origin increases.

The information above does not reveal the way these strategies interact, nor does it reveal the complexity of how these strategies chain together in stressful environments, nor how they 'marry' between two or more people. The word in parentheses at the end of each cluster indicates the primary 'emotion' that the role is intended to banish from experience by taking on these ways of being in the world.

As an example, a Family Hero strategy may be the strategy that I am most effective at running. I've learned over time that how I am most effective in my world; how I am most valued in my experience is by moving through the world demonstrating the behaviours of a Family Hero. I become very good at all the things that Family Hero's do. It may well be that I do that until I begin to notice that I am not producing the result that I desire and will then shift to either a Lost Child strategy and remove myself from my environment by isolating, or perhaps a Scapegoat strategy and will remove myself by getting drunk.

These profiles are not who we are! They represent how we do things and what we do as ways of responding to people, events and circumstances in our lives. It is common for the children in a family system to take on one of these as their preferred way of interacting in their family. It is also very common for these profiles to change over time, sometimes taking turns and shifting as one member of the family takes over for another. It is also very common for a member of the family to engage one strategy at home (i.e. Family Hero) and another at work (i.e. Lost Child), with strategies changing with circumstances.

These profiles are not who we are!

There is intelligence in the way we move through our days. Engaging in these predictable clusters of behavior makes it possible for us to respond to our lives automatically, demonstrating ways that are repetitious, and makes it possible for people to 'know' us. You'll often hear things like "So-and-so is the smart one" or "So-and-so is the loser" and what is really being talked about is how we've labeled people by the behavioral clusters that they've come to rely on as an automatic response to their environment.

We are not our strategies! We are not fixed in our potential nor limited in our ability to express the uniqueness of who we are. However, these family roles/behavioral profiles which I believe are strategies or habituated ways for living effectively, can (over time) even seem to us to be who we are. We do ourselves a great disservice when we do not allow ourselves to go beyond these habits of thought and mind and explore the underlying ground that not only spawns them but that also makes it possible for us to change them.

We are not fixed in our potential nor limited in our ability to express the uniqueness of who we are

Who we grow up to be has much more to do with who we're told we are than it does with anything else. Growing up in our families of origin defines who we become – unless we say otherwise!

Putting the patterns in place

We are voracious learning machines. We are never *not* learning. The organic, intelligent, living system that we are is always gathering information. The question is, given that we are always gathering information, what are we learning… to do… to be… to become?

In addition to the basic data of the experiences of being human, over time these experiences generalize to world-views that are held in place by sets of beliefs, values and attitudes. These, too, we learn in our family of origin.

Before we go on, I would like to note – for the record – that I am well aware of the sanctity with which society holds the family. I do not believe that this system, any more or less than any other, is beyond the scope of our curiosity and observation. For far too long, scrutiny of the family system has been taboo, out of bounds and too sacred to be held up for review or placed under the microscope of our evolving awareness. For far too long, children have been considered the property of their parents, sometimes at the mercy of them and to do with as they please.

For far too long, scrutiny of the family system has been taboo

Our children are the future. I believe that it's time to look at the fundamental system from which all other systems evolve; the first system that stands as the model for and sets the standards by which all subsequent systems will be structured and judged. This early family system holds immense power to shape and mold us at a time in our lives when we are without the freedom to choose. When you're five, you can't get a job and leave

This early family system holds immense power to shape and mold us at a time in our lives when we are without the freedom to choose town. As we grow, this changes if and when we become able to recognize that we are now capable of changing it and can do so by choice. As children, this freedom does not exist.

As we become better informed about and aware of the degree to which those early family system experiences shape the structure of subsequent living systems – *not only for the individual but for our capacity to structure the systems themselves!* – we become more able to embrace what we have created and choose to create again, differently. We become able to move away from our need to judge and find fault and to blame, and to simply notice that if something of our own creation isn't producing the result we desire, we can decide what we want instead and change it. If we do not explore and understand this with more clarity and depth of awareness, all we can do is repeat what we know which is the parent/child model.

Historically and typically, this model is based on the need to control and to contain; on the need to make people do things. Perhaps a useful model at one time, it does not serve us today, be it in our corporate environments, our educational environments or our religious systems, to name a few. The command-and-control model of our early family systems no longer supports and sustains life.

The command-and-control model of our early family systems no longer supports and sustains life

I no longer believe that what I carry with me from my past is baggage or garbage, although that has not always been the case. The accumulation of my past experiences, like yours, not only have brought me to where I am today but have also allowed me to learn, grow and become more proficient at being uniquely who I am. There is nothing going on inside of me that belongs to anyone but me. The mind-boggling efficiency of the nervous system implies that it must exist for some purpose.

There is nothing going on inside of me that belongs to anyone but me

What I carry inside me that produces bodily responses (or feelings) in me is one thing and one thing only: information. Coming face-to-face with and embracing this information is crucial to my capacity to heal, to grow, to build and to evolve. If I continue to think of this information/these feelings as the enemy or as toxic waste, why on earth would I want to embrace or lay claim to any of it? And yet if I don't claim it, how can I learn from it? And worse, it will claim me.

Why would we be surprised that we are creating work environments that reflect the parent/child model? We all come from some version of an original family system. We leave those systems and do what we've been taught to do, think what we've been taught to think and become who we've been shaped to become. (I've come to conclude from my experiences and from what I've witnessed over the years in working with others that the only reason work exists is so that we all have someplace to go to work out our unresolved family issues!) We then take this information (because that's all it is, information) and mindlessly or in a habituated fashion, go about doing what we know how to do: interacting with each other based on those family patterns; rarely, if ever, telling the truth as we know it inside ourselves if it is in conflict with what we have been taught to hold as 'truth'. Though we sometimes make minor adjustments for keeping up with the times, these are replicated systems nonetheless.

As we grow up in these early family systems, we take on the beliefs, values and attitudes of the authority/power figures in our experience. Why? Because it's the smart thing to do given that it's all we know and we have no leverage to do otherwise. It's not a good thing or a bad thing, a right thing or a wrong thing – it just is. If we are not aware of this, we tend to experience these structures as 'reality' or what we know we know (Figure 1). So deeply ingrained is much of it that we never consider that there might be something else, until we get into our late 30's to early 50's. Around that time, we begin to get a sense that something's missing and we're not quite sure what it is.

What's missing is us! Our individuality, our uniqueness, our connection to something deep inside us that makes us want to get out of bed in the morning and face life with a full heart and an open mind. We begin to notice that our commitment, often one that has been life long, to what's outside of us (the rules, the regulations, the status quo, and other people's expectations) hasn't delivered on its promise of contentment and serenity. We begin to ache for something that we lost long, long ago and don't quite know where to start looking to rediscover it.

What's missing is us! Our individuality, our uniqueness, our connection to something deep inside us that makes us want to get out of bed in the morning and face life with a full heart and an open mind

Redefining work

When was the last time we considered *how* we think about work/life? We just assume we already know. After all, we were raised with the cultural mantra of: grow up, get an education, get a job; grow up, get an education, get a job. We do what our parents before us have done. We habitually and mindlessly, without conscious thought, reproduce work environments that will fit into the context that we have been conditioned into. (Imagine what we do in the parenting department….) We don't think about it, we simply do it. To do otherwise is to be labeled disruptive: a rebel, a troublemaker and worse. We turn ourselves into a pretzel trying to conform to others' expectations of us, knowing full well we have neither interest nor desire to live our lives that way. Why, then, are we amazed at the rate of 'addiction' or 'depression' in our culture? You cannot cut yourself off from your own internal awareness for an extended period of time without having to find a way to stop the pain.

When was the last time we considered how we think about work/life?

But what if the potential that work holds is much greater than what we've been taught? From a living systems perspective, work isn't a place you go to or even a thing that you do. It's an experience you create – moment to moment to moment – from the inside of you based on your beliefs, values and attitudes about yourself (that first conversation) and about the other individuals around you (your conversation with another human being). We are not victims to it nor are we at the mercy of it. We are its architects and we can change it in the blink of an eye.

We are the creators of what we already have. Perhaps not by mindful intention and design but the creators nonetheless. For many of us, we would prefer to think that someone else did this and we are victims to it; that it's 'not my fault'; that we're hard done by and overpowered by something much greater than we are. Much of the way that people think in today's work/life environments is that they are victims to a much larger force and they stand on the 'effect' side of the equation.

You can think like that if you choose but be mindful that you are choosing nonetheless. Every choice has its natural consequences. Be mindful that every time you say yes when you want to say no, you keep the system in place. Every time you participate in something that feels wrong to you, you keep the system in place. Your every action in some way moves the system in some direction. What direction are you going in?

Be mindful that every time you say yes when you want to say no, you keep the system in place. Every time you participate in something that feels wrong to you, you keep the system in place

Open and closed loops

The list of characteristics referred to in *Figure 2* represent the experience of a Closed Loop System (*Figure 3*). They are also the behavioral characteristics that pervade our early family systems as well as every other living system that we participate in, including religious, corporate and educational systems. Why?

Simple - because that's what we know how to do. We have grown up in systems where these behavioral characteristics were present on a daily basis and we've learned how to survive in them. We have even come not only to take these on as our own, but have developed personal favorites along the way. A couple of mine were perfectionism and crisis orientation. Maybe a couple of yours include blame or resentment, or maybe shame and guilt. Doesn't really matter which ones you've gotten good at, they all have the effect of keeping the system small and tight. The bottom line is that they are all driven by fear of pain in some way – humiliation, loss, dismissal, physical assault or being left out. We learn very early how to best protect ourselves from these experiences.

These characteristics are also referred to as the characteristics of a dead system or an addictive system. They represent the behaviors of a practicing addict as defined more than 60 years ago by Alcoholics Anonymous. We know that if addicts continue to do their addiction, they die. When these same behaviors pervade our work environments, why would we be surprised or puzzled when we find our organizational systems (all around the globe) are dying; are collapsing in on themselves and not supporting life? Just like the individual addicted system (practicing alcoholic) eventually succumbs, the same principles that apply to one level of the system will repeat at other levels of the system.

Why would we be surprised or puzzled when we find our organizational systems (all around the globe) are dying; are collapsing in on themselves and not supporting life?

There is no shortage of books that you can read on family systems and the implications of addiction. We have already seen how, as children, we take on these patterns in early years as a way of finding our place in the family system with the intention of navigating through it with a sense of safety and well-being. Once these patterns are in place, we begin to think it's who we are. We take these patterns everywhere we go, including work, and interact accordingly. Sometimes, before we can begin to allow ourselves to notice that it's not working for us anymore, our lives have to fall apart. Work is already falling apart with a very real call to creating something much more supportive of the individual.

In our high-tech world, people are finding ways to leave large corporate systems. They are starting small businesses from their basements; moving to other corporate systems that offer not just money but time with the family. At a recent luncheon with a well-respected female executive as the keynote speaker, I was struck by her lamenting the degree to which executive women are leaving corporate (North) America – in droves. She expressed deep concern about this. Her belief was that it was essential for these women to stay and in so doing, these systems would change. What came to mind for me was how, at other levels of the culture, women feel an obligation or a sense of duty to stay in 'family' situations (be they family of origin or corporate) that are killing them – sometimes emotionally, spiritually or physically. Not only do women feel this obligation but other women are quick to hold them to it as doing 'the right thing', culturally conditioned to be the caretakers of the relationships, often at the cost of their own well-being. Here was another example of women doing the same old thing, one more time, and the only thing that had changed was the address.

Here was another example of women doing the same old thing, one more time, and the only thing that had changed was the address

My personal belief is that nothing will change those systems faster than for people to leave them, create other systems that offer something different and life-sustaining and allow nature to take its course in bringing the other system to its inevitable end. To continue to force ourselves, from a sense of 'duty' or 'obligation', to undertake heroics to save a system that fundamentally does not support life in its basic design only postpones the inevitable, natural consequence.

We are not stuck with what we have. We have what it takes to move on and create something else. But if we believe that the system we have is the way it is (learned early in life), then we will think that there's nothing we can do about it. Witness the exodus of women from corporate America, resulting in more than 89% of small businesses, which employ more people than all the Fortune 500's combined, being led by women. Sometimes the best thing to do is just to walk away. In so doing, it's a wake-up call that is loud enough to be heard by those who remain.

We can't give away what doesn't belong to us. Nor can we change what's not ours. Before we can make a difference at work, we must reclaim what's there. We must accept that we did it. All of it. The parts we like and the parts we don't. We did it by the things we said and the ones we didn't say. We did it by the times we took action and the times we sat back in silence, waiting for someone else to do the job. We did it by saying that we had no choice because we need the paycheck when what we really meant was that we'd have to learn something new or become someone different or take some personal risks before we could walk away. We did it by pretending that someone else would fix it – someone outside - with a policy paper, a mission statement or a piece of legislation. But whatever we've got, we did it. That doesn't mean it's what we deserve, it's just what we knew how to do. The question now becomes: *what do we want to do instead?*

Wě can't give away what doesn't belong to us. Nor can we change what's not ours. Before we can make a difference at work, we must reclaim what's there

For more information, consider:

- *Quantum Healing* by Deepak Chopra
- *Molecules of Emotion* by Candace Pert
- *Infinite Mind: The Vibrations of Human Consciousness* by Valerie Hunt
- *The Psychobiology of Mind-Body Healing* by Ernest Rossi
- *The Scientific Foundation of Hypnotherapy* by Bruce Lipton
- *Jaguar Woman* by Lynn Andrews
- *Wheels of Life* by Anodea Judith
- *Breaking Down the Wall of Silence* by Alice Miller
- *The Biology of Belief* by Bruce Lipton

FULLY ALIVE

The problems of today cannot be resolved at the same level of thinking that created them.

- Albert Einstein -

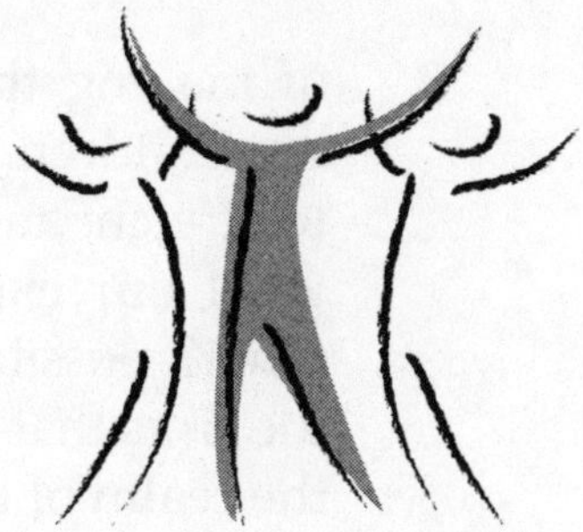

CHAPTER 5

Choosing It

What do we want instead?

When it comes to work, we know what we want. We want to know what respect and dignity and integrity *feel* like inside our bodies and not just have philosophical discussions about them, or put them on a to-do list for the next mission statement. We want to know that our being at work makes a difference; that we contribute and that our opinions and ideas are useful and valid. We want to know that it matters whether or not we show up; and that someone notices when we don't. We want to *feel* good about what we do, how we do it and the people we do it with. We want *truth* to be a part of our daily routines and not something that we blurt out when we can't stand it anymore. We want to be able to care deeply about ourselves and each other, knowing that there's nothing going on at work but us, and that everything else will be a reflection of how well we understand and honor that. We want to *feel* alive and authentic in the things we say and do.

We want to create work environments that support and sustain life; that invite health, humor, compassion and truth. We want to take part in creating something greater than ourselves: be part of something where the whole is greater than the sum of the parts; a place where magic and miracles are a part of life. We want to be part of making the world a better place for ourselves and our children. We want to be able to grow and expand; to stretch; and finally, to spread our wings and fly. We want our experience of flight to stand as a model of what's possible and as testimony to our courage to take the risks that will bring joy, vitality and delight back into the realm of day-to-day living.

We want to be able to breathe deeply; to relax and to laugh; to create and bring new ideas and approaches and opportunities into the light of day. We want to share. We want to open ourselves to new experiences and create them for others, without the fear of being ridiculed or humiliated or dismissed. We want to be able to have work be part of our complete life process and have room for our families and our friends, without the fear of being marginalized or made irrelevant.

How do we get where we want to go? Who do we need to become in order for us to be able to create these environments for ourselves and each other? What context do we need to create that will be big enough, dynamic enough and vital enough to be able to support the enormity of who we are capable of becoming - at work, at home and in the communities in which we live?

Where do we begin?

Where do we start to make a difference in what it feels like to get up and go to work on Monday morning? The answer is simple and not necessarily easy.

We start... with something that transcends philosophy and principle and dogma. We start with you and me

We start with what's really there; with what's not a nominalization and that you *can* put in the trunk of your car; with something that transcends philosophy and principle and dogma; with something that exists in space and time. We start with the individual human beings in their individual human bodies with their individual and very human feelings. We start with you and me.

Getting conscious is the key. Conscious, as an adjective, is described as:

- "Having an awareness of one's own existence, sensations, and thoughts, and of one's environment". I would take that one step further and I would say having an awareness of one's own sensations and thoughts and *trusting* this information enough to be willing to act on it and express it.
- "Capable of complex response to an environment" – and this complexity unfolds simply, from moment to moment, like the small incremental changes that ultimately, together, create the powerful expressions of nature that we have come to call hurricanes; rather than trying to decipher from the outset what the master plan will be.
- "Not asleep; awake" – and being willing to trust that you see what you see, you hear what you hear and you know what you know. Being truly awake also means that your reality, as you structure it, is just as valid to you as mine is to me. To argue this is a moot point; to respect it builds tolerance and compassion; to embrace it and dive into it brings creativity and innovation into our daily, mundane, humdrum existences.
- "Subjectively known" – as opposed to objectively analyzed and assessed; and run by everybody you know who you think is smarter and tougher than you, so they can tell you what you know!
- "Intentionally conceived or done; deliberate" – as in mindful, purposeful.

Other words that could be used to describe the notion of 'conscious' are alive, alert and aware.

Getting conscious!

To facilitate our journey into conscious choosing so that we may allow ourselves to consider the possibilities and then choose with an open mind and a courageous spirit; and given that we would like to ponder our choice from a higher level of thinking than that which has created our current experience and its accompanying attempts at resolution, it would be useful to have a framework for processing that information.

We already know that the human body is a magnificent bio-computer. We also know that the central nervous system allows us to *think* or process information in a number of ways. The nervous system is actually so dense that if everything else were to be removed from the body – all the bones, organs, muscle, etc. - you would still be recognizable as who you are. Small wonder that you would have sensory responses in the body when the nervous system is processing an experience. You call it a *feeling*.

Think of this sensory experience in your body as equivalent to a blinking light on your computer

We know from science that information moves through the body via biochemical and electrochemical impulses that allow the cells to transfer information or 'chat'. These 'chats' are critical to maintaining health and well-being; with our immune system listening in attentively on the conversations we have with ourselves, i.e. psychoneuroimmunology. Think of this sensory experience in your body as equivalent to a blinking light on your computer. When the light is blinking, you think that's a good thing and that you will benefit from the experience when it is complete. However, when you're body is processing information – when you're having a feeling and your internal light is blinking – you often stop the process.

Based on what you've been taught to believe *about* feelings - whether they're good or bad and which ones you're allowed to have and which ones you aren't – you may pull the plug on your internal computer to stop the processing. How you do that is by holding your breath or by distracting yourself with something else (maybe food, booze, sex, gambling, work) so that you lose awareness of the feeling as it's moving through your body. That's not a good thing or a bad thing – it's just the way we do it.

The purpose of feelings

When it comes to emotions, we are a culture that has become insane! Just stop for a moment and think of what happens to you when you begin to cry – particularly in public. Or what happens to you when someone else begins to cry in front of you? Do you find yourself running for the hills? Trying to fix everything so that the tears will stop? Or do you just go numb and pretend that none of it is happening. After all, there's nothing going on except some water in someone's eyes or on their cheeks. We have however, been taught to attach meaning to the movement of this water, based on our culturally conditioned sets of beliefs, and we then make interpretations and judgments about the experience of the tears and act accordingly.

We know there's nothing going on at work but individual human beings having conversations inside themselves and with each other. What you call f*eelings* are a naturally occurring phenomenon that accompanies the movement of information through the body, with the movement of this information being called *thinking*. In order for us to stop feeling at work, we also have to stop thinking! Isn't this exactly what we've done,

In order for us to stop feeling at work, we also have to stop thinking!

with the alternative to thinking being simply to repeat habits? And isn't this result exactly what's causing us problems – at work and elsewhere?

Think of your feelings as messengers in a bottle; or messengers from inner space, as Dr. Chopra would say. When you're feeling a feeling, think of the sensory response in your body as being the wave that moves through the individual living system that you are that carries the information in the bottle to where it needs to go to make a difference in your life. Along comes the wave, bringing the bottle with its new insight for you or its layer of awareness and before you even get to read the message, you squash the whole thing because you have been taught not to like the waves. In your effort to stop the waves, you (often unwittingly) give up the message itself. Over time, your life becomes an on-going effort to stop the waves, becoming ever mindless about the messages that are now accumulating, waiting to be delivered. With the passage of time will frequently come an increasing intensity of the swells. And sometimes, we explode.

Imagine, just for a moment, a different scenario. Imagine being a little boy or a little girl and being in the presence of adults who value and respect their own internal messages. When a wave moves through you, someone stays with you, looks you in the eyes and says the kinds of things that you need to hear to let you know that: a) you're supposed to have waves; that waves are normal and very important; and that those waves are a sign of life to be welcomed and celebrated; and that those waves carry the information that will distinguish you from everyone else on the planet; b) that the waves carry bottles with messages; and c) here's one of the many ways to welcome the bottles and decode the messages. What would life have been like if we had been taught to judge those waves as being signals of impending growth and expansion; a sign of a new level of magnificence; of being pathways to becoming powerful in our expression both internally and externally? I wonder who we would have become….

Work and feelings

There is a direct relationship between the process of thinking and the experience of feeling. Both 'thinking' and 'feeling' are nominalizations. The only thing that is 'real' is the sensory response in the tissue of the body. When we shut down those responses in the body, we don't prevent the information from moving; we just prevent ourselves from having any conscious awareness of what the information carries. We develop and perfect, over time, a capacity for denying the experience of the self (or self-denial) which eventually leaves us not knowing who we are: what we care about, what we want and where we are trying to go. In addition, this state of denial of what is moving through us and inside us leaves us looking outside of ourselves for guidance and direction. We become dependent on referring to what's already there - the rules and regulations and expectations - and then we don't understand why we feel separate and disenfranchised; why things don't seem real to us or like they don't belong to us. *It's because they don't.*

There is a direct relationship between the process of thinking and the experience of feeling

Like hamsters on a wheel, we go 'round and 'round, desperately trying to avoid the sensory responses in the body by repeating things that we know, the things that we've been taught to do, the things that we are told will make life better; hoping that life will change. It doesn't. We come to feel cheated and taken advantage of. And nobody has done this to us - we do it to ourselves.

We come to feel cheated and taken advantage of. And nobody has done this to us - we do it to ourselves

Without the capacity to honor our feelings at work, we have no choice but to give up thinking. What passes for thinking today is really nothing more than habit. Remember those 65,000 thoughts a day, more than 90%

of them the same as you thought yesterday? What a waste of a magnificent instrument! It's like having a Lear Jet and insisting on driving along the highways, from one place to the other. The only limitations on our potential are the ones we impose upon ourselves.

The only limitations on our potential are the ones we impose upon ourselves

Feelings and thinking

In addition to actually moving information through its neural pathways, the nervous system organizes that information in a way that holds meaning for us and that we can access when we need/want it. One tool that helps us to know what we need to know in order to access this information in a practical way is The Iceberg of the Self™ *(Figure 6).*

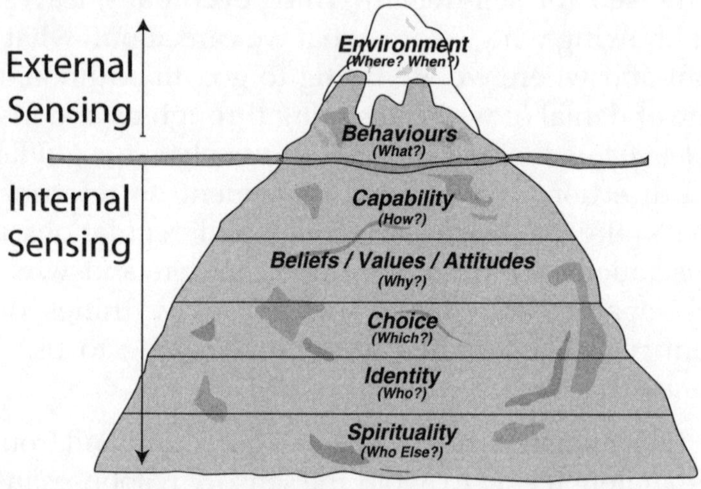

Figure 6: Iceberg of the Self™

Based on some of the work originally developed by Gregory Bateson (cybernetic theory) and expanded by Robert Dilts (Neuro-Linguistic Programming), The Iceberg has evolved from this original work that is often referred to as Logical Levels of Thinking *(Figure 7).* This model allows us to better understand *how* we process information and to bring the *structure of thought* to conscious awareness so that we may choose with intention and mindfulness. It arranges the information from levels, or clusters, of the very specific (level of Environment) to the very general (level of Spirituality). In this way, we can direct our attention (think of attention as the flashlight of your awareness or consciousness) to any level we choose and access the information at that level. We can choose to direct our thinking to any (higher or lower) level of thought, depending on what we want to achieve.

Spirituality
(Who Else?)

Identity
(Who?)

Beliefs/Values/Attitudes
(Why?)

Capability (Strategy)
(How?)

Behavior
(What?)

Environment
(Where, When?)

Figure 7: Logical Levels of Thinking

David Bohm, a brilliant theoretical physicist, believed that thought, itself, was a system. Happy to say that I'm in good company when I share that belief. Thought is, indeed, a system that can be understood and worked with; a system that can be managed and directed once we know how. The Iceberg of the Self™ is a tool that will help us to do that. But I'm getting ahead of myself…

Back to the Logical Levels of Thinking. As developed by Bateson and Dilts, there are six Logical Levels of Thinking, ranging from Environment (at the very bottom) to Spirituality (at the very top). Each of these levels is identifiable by the nature of the questions to which the level would respond. For example, at the level of Environment, the things that you would be thinking/talking/writing about would respond to questions about where and/or when. At the Behavior level, they would respond to questions about what. And so on, up the ladder.

The most important thing to be aware of with Logical Levels is that each level is contained in and driven by the level above it. So, if my thinking is currently at the Behavior level and I want to make a change at that level, to be effective I would have to raise my thinking to at least one level above it – Capability – and explore *how* else I could express myself to achieve the result I want.

A crucial thing to notice about these Logical Levels is that the first two levels at the bottom – Environment and Behavior – allow for external sensing. That means that I can use my external senses to gather factual information (sensory based, behaviorally specific) about you.

> Your external senses are the ones that allow you to gather information from the outside of you. Internal sensing allows you to notice the things that are only inside of you, like the pictures you make inside yourself, or the things you say to yourself, or the internal filters of your beliefs, values or attitudes that you carry inside you. The only way that another person can authentically know anything from the inside of you is if you choose to share it with them.

You can use this external sensing process to gather information at these levels. For example, external sensing allows me to notice that as I sit in a room and know that it's Tuesday at 4:00 p.m., I can also look at you and know that you're there too, on Tuesday at 4:00 p.m. I can gather that information about you because that information *about* you exists outside of you, too. However, I can sit in my chair and know *why* I'm there (my beliefs, values and attitudes which are inside me, at a higher level of thinking) but I can't know those things for sure about you just by using my external sensing. (I can make them up – which we're very prone to do!) If I really want to know that about you, the only way I can know for sure is to include you in the conversation and ask.

Unlike Maslow's *Hierarchy of Needs*, Logical Levels are not dependent one upon the other for upward movement. We cycle through all levels on a regular basis. Although the Identity Level may be very useful for me to focus my attention on when I'm parenting my children, it may be more useful (not to mention practical and safe!) for me to focus my attention at the Environment Level when I'm crossing a busy street. I'll live longer that way.

Using Logical Levels of Thinking is a very powerful tool that brings the structure of thought to conscious awareness. In this way, we can work with that system rather than have it run amok in our lives. Like your body creates a new stomach lining for you every four days – whether you do anything about it or not – thought also has a structure that it follows and a system through which it flows, whether you are aware of it or not. It will simply do what it's designed to do. Sometimes it will work for you - and sometimes it won't.

Thought also has a structure that it follows and a system through which it flows, whether you are aware of it or not

Without your conscious awareness of how thought as a system operates, and without your conscious intention to direct it, sometimes thought will get you where you want to go and sometimes thought will take you in another direction, or just leave you standing where you are, going around in circles. Isn't it nice to know that you can make choices about all this?

Understanding the concept of Logical Levels of Thinking helps us to comprehend that if we want to make a change in the quality of our lives – at work, at home or elsewhere – the degree to which we will be able to produce this result will be the degree to which we can work the levers of thought. The higher up I go in my levels of thinking; the more I am willing to entertain the larger and larger questions, the greater the impact in my life.

As we move up the levels of thinking, given that each level is contained in the level above it, change at any level will automatically affect all of the levels below it. That means that if I make a change at a high level of thinking like Beliefs, Values and Attitudes, everything below it will change all by itself – and that includes my behaviors. No need for struggle, will power and determination unless you believe it to be necessary. In that case, like Henry Ford said, "If you think you can, or if you think you can't, you're right." It's up to you.

Consider, as an example, what it was like for you when you were four and you believed in Santa Clause. Remember what it was like on Christmas Eve? There you were, padding around the house in your jammies with the little feet in them, nose pressed up against the window, mesmerized by the magic of the falling snow; listening for sounds of reindeer hooves and sleigh bells on the roof. You were so eager for Santa to arrive that you could hardly stand it; and you were even willing to go to bed early, thinking that the sooner you went to sleep the faster he'd get here!

Fast forward – and now you're ten. You don't believe in Santa anymore. Now, as Christmas approaches, you find yourself fighting your siblings for the Sears

Wishbook because you know that if you don't get there first, there will be so many pages missing you might lose out. You also start working on your mother around October so that she gets lots of advance notice and will have the time to find what you want. Instead of padding around in your jammies with the feet in them, nosed pressed up against the window, you now prowl the house in stocking feet, waiting for an opportunity to invade the closets so that you can shake the boxes and peel back the corners on the wrapping, just to get a quick peek. On Christmas day, you'd just as soon sleep in since you already know everything that's under the tree, anyway.

A very different set of experiences. And yet, the only thing that changed was your belief. You'll notice that when you're belief changed at age ten, you didn't have to sit down and make a list of how your behaviors should now change accordingly. It just happened. All by itself. Effortlessly.

The same potential for effortless change exists in other ways, too. Say, for example, that you want to quit smoking. If at the level of Identity your hold yourself to be a smoker, you can turn yourself inside out at the lower level of Behavior and you'll still want to smoke. Why? Because you believe you're a smoker. Or, you may actually succeed in not smoking but find yourself craving cigarettes, feeling angry and resentful about not smoking. Why? Because now, you're a *deprived* smoker.

If you want to quit smoking effortlessly, change your Identity first. There are now ways of intervening at these higher levels of thinking (see tools in Changing It). These, of course, will challenge your thinking in other ways, particularly your beliefs about change, itself. We've been brought up to believe that change is hard; that it takes a long time; that you really have to work at it; that you're going to have to struggle and use willpower and determination; and that if you get change without all of this, it won't last or it won't be worthwhile. You can live your life that way if you want to, but remember that you are choosing all the way.

The 7th Logical Level

Throughout this material, we've given the process of choice a lot of attention. Most of us have grown up in and continue to evolve in family, educational, community, religious and work environments that did not then and do not now encourage individual, original thinking. And yet, without the experience of choosing something of our own creation, we are not really choosing at all but facing a range of options created by someone else. Authentic choice must involve me directly as the creator of my own experience.

Authentic choice must involve me directly as the creator of my own experience

I believe deeply in the power of the process of choice. As such, I've added a seventh level to the work already done by Bateson and Dilts – the Logical Level of Choice *(Figure 8)*. Without having a place where we can stand – consciously – and with mindfulness and purposefulness define what we want, it becomes far too easy for us to experience ourselves as victims; to find ourselves on the effect side of the equation because the process of choosing is one that has become transparent to us. That it's transparent does not mean that it's absent.

Think of the structure of all seven of these Logical Levels as lining up and equating with the passage of time.

PAST -------------------	NOW -------------------	FUTURE
Environment	Choice	Identity
Behavior		Spirituality
Capability		
Beliefs/Values/Attitudes		

Spirituality
(Who Else?)

Identity
(Who?)

Choice
(Which?)

Beliefs/Values/Attitudes
(Why?)

Capability (Strategy)
(How?)

Behavior
(What?)

Environment
(Where, When?)

Figure 8: Predictable Structure of Thought

The lower levels of Environment, Behavior, Capability and Beliefs/Values/Attitudes would equate with the past. All of the information associated to these levels would relate to that which you've already been taught or that you've already done. Think of the higher logical levels of Identity and Spirituality as equating with the future, with the potential of who you are capable of becoming; with what's possible for you as an individual human being and as a member of a larger collective. Then consider the level of Choice as the bridge that stands between the past and the future; as the point of the perpetual NOW from which you choose, moment to moment; choosing to repeat the past

Consider the level of Choice as the bridge that stands between the past and the future (what you already know) or to move boldly into the future (what you don't know you don't know, or the domain of all that's possible).

A conscious awareness of the point of Choice allows you to stay mindful that every response has a naturally occurring consequence which will take you in one direction or another. It also keeps you mindful that although your thoughts can travel through time – remembering the past or imagining the future - your body is always in the present, moving from moment to moment, with your body as the instrument of expression in that perpetual now.

The sensory responses that move through your body as it stands in the NOW will give you the information and the guidance that you are looking for and require in order to continue to move through time; to know how to choose the path of your preferred existence. What direction do you want to go in? Do you want to create something new or repeat what's already there? To what degree are you willing to take conscious action in the creation of your own life? Do you choose to stand on the Cause side or the Effect side of the equation? The choice is always yours.

The Iceberg of The Self™

Back in the early '90's, when I first began to work with this material in a corporate setting, I had the opportunity to work with a client group of about 30 people. Having shared this information with them, they were quite enthused about its potential, particularly in a group/team building process, and went eagerly about putting it to use on a day-to-day basis. A handout of this model was either pinned to the wall or sat on the desk of those people who had attended our program. It was also on the wall of the meeting room so that they could be reminded of another way to communicate with each other – not as dogma but as a possibility. Within a week or two, we discovered that some of our clients were having difficulty because they "...could not stay at that high 'Spirituality' level all the time". Did we have any advice for them?

Stop for a moment and consider the culturally conditioned associations with what we would call a ladder (i.e. a structure of one thing on top of another). The implication is that there is a progression - that the top is better than the bottom - and that when you climb the ladder of success, where you want to be is at the top! Some of our clients had come to think of the top (Spirituality) as an indication of where they should always have their attention.

In order to create a different representation of the information that these levels of thinking could make available, we restructured the information into The Iceberg of The Self™ *(Figure 6)* with Environment and Behavior above the water line and accessible to external sensing; and everything else below the water line. Like the Titanic, we all know that what often will sink something (a plan, an intention, a goal, a dream) is what's below the water line.

Each of us lives in one of these Icebergs *(Figure 9)*. You sit in yours and I sit in mine, and we go merrily about the business of life. Where we get into trouble is that as I sit in my Iceberg noticing things about you that are above the water line, I am not content simply to be an observer to that experience. I then take that information, drop into my Iceberg – into my Beliefs, Values and Attitudes - and make judgments about you based on those beliefs, and come to conclusions about you – all without ever consulting you.

For example, let's pretend for a moment that I am doing a presentation to a group of people and you happen to be in the room. As I stand at the front of the room, talking and making notes on a flip chart, or moving through a series of slides, you get up and walk out of the room. Without missing a beat, I continue to talk and share information with the rest of the group (we are all designed to multi-task!) while inside me, I begin a conversation that goes something like this: "The nerve!! Imagine walking out in the middle of what I'm saying! Obviously, s/he has no manners and is very unprofessional!"

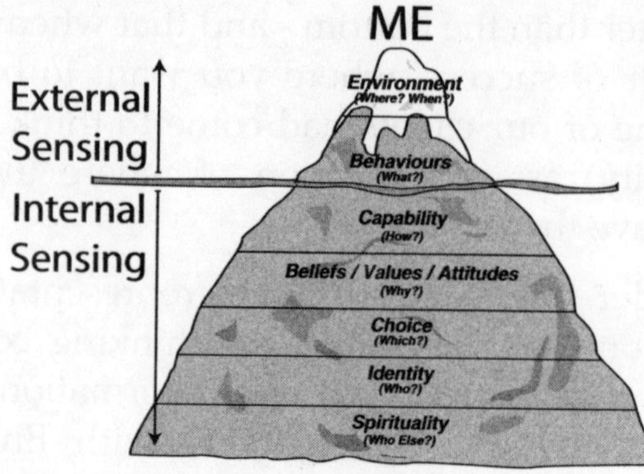

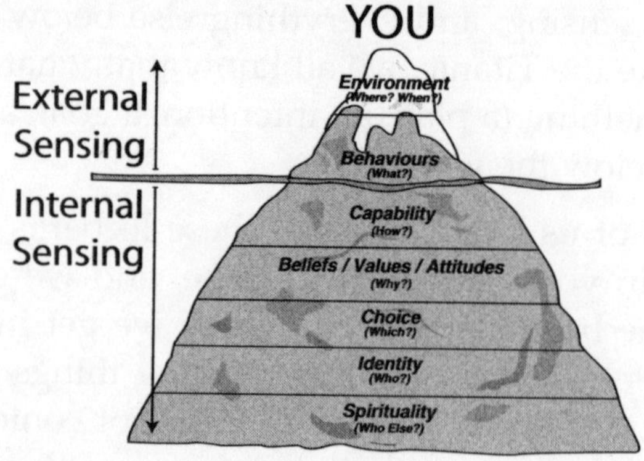

Figure 9: Icebergs Interacting

The entire time that I'm talking to you, I'm also talking to myself.

The things I have to say about you are bad enough. But I go a little bit deeper inside myself and I also observe: "Well, maybe if I were more interesting, he/she wouldn't be able to leave the room." Now, I've made a judgment about you but, at a deeper level, I've also made a judgment about myself. How do you think I'm going to feel about you when you come back into the room? How do you think I'm going to respond to you when you ask me a question about the very material that I covered while you were out of the room? Highly unlikely that I'll be 'warm and fuzzy'. All that turmoil inside me – and maybe all you did was use the washroom, or check with a babysitter.

My judgments about you, just like your judgments about me, have nothing to do with you. They are a reflection of what's inside me. My judgments about you or anything else reveal volumes about who I am; what I believe and value; and how I think. My judgments about you are a statement about me which I then package into words and reveal to the world – if you know how to listen. Someone once wrote a book called "What You Think of Me is None of My Business". Now you know why that's true.

My judgments about you have nothing to do with you. They are a reflection of what's inside me

Place a copy of The Iceberg of the Self™ where you can see it. Keep one on your fridge door or under your desk blotter or even on your bathroom mirror, as a reminder that you reveal yourself, from moment to moment, through your observations and judgments. You may begin to notice things about yourself that, so far, have escaped you but are very obvious to those around you. You may want to begin to notice what others already know.

Work Environments as Living Systems® or WEL-Systems®

Before we can move on to other things; before we can begin to create something different for ourselves and the people we spend time with, it may be useful to *know what we want to create.* Given what we now know, we can stand on the Cause side of the equation and choose to create consciously; or we can continue to stand on the Effect side of the equation and consider ourselves to be victims in the process. If we do not consciously choose for ourselves, the larger systems in which we live will unfold in accordance with the choices that someone else will make for us. If we do not stand on the Cause side of the equation and choose for ourselves, someone else will choose for us and may well use us as resources in the accomplishment of their goals or intentions. Either way, we will have chosen, even if what we've chosen is to not choose.

If we do not stand on the Cause side of the equation and choose for ourselves, someone else will choose for us

Perhaps the greatest opportunity that now stands before us in the world of corporate life is one that unfolds at many levels, simultaneously. And yes, we are up to that task! Not only do we now know that we can choose consciously, we also know that we can choose to *move our thinking* to any level and choose from and within any of those levels. Choices within choices within choices.....

We can stand on the Cause side of the equation and choose to consciously create at the Environment level or we can stand on the Cause side of the equation and choose to consciously create at the Identity level. It's up to us. The higher up you go with the levels of thinking, the greater the potential of your own creation – and the fewer the details you will have.

At the higher levels of thinking, you will be addressing the nature of identity, as well as the structure of beliefs, values and attitudes. At the lower levels, you will be considering information that would respond to questions about where, when and what. Specifics at these lower levels of thinking are much easier to discern since you will be extracting that information with external sensing and will be focused on things that already exist. At the higher levels of thinking, you will be focused on bringing into existence that which does not yet exist. You can appreciate that the details may be lacking!

At the lower levels of thinking, your creations will have definition and specifics. At the higher levels, they will have direction and intention, requiring that you fully engage the process, from moment to moment. You will need to develop mastery of the discomfort that comes with living in uncertainty. How you choose to create your experience is entirely up to you. (Refer to *Phoenix Rising: The Freeing of Human Potential* for more on The CODE Model™ - CODE means Creation Out of Deep Energy - and how to use logical levels or the structure of your thoughts in tandem with the experiences in your body or the chakras/energy centers, to decode the messages as they move through your awareness.)

You will need to develop mastery of the discomfort that comes with living in uncertainty

Work Environments as Living Systems® or WEL-Systems® is *an approach* to or context for organizational, professional and personal change that evolved from the work that I'd been doing with clients since 1990. A WEL-Systems approach engages you at a very high level of thinking (Identity and Spirituality) and creates a context, or a world-view, within which the subsequent choices at the lower levels can unfold in a way that supports those higher intentions.

A WEL-Systems approach engages you at a very high level of thinking

The WEL-Systems approach to change recognizes that *all meaning is context dependent*; that the only thing going on at work – and everywhere else! - is individual human beings interacting with other individual human beings; and that the natural state of being human is to grow and contribute. With this in mind, the WEL-Systems™ approach to change is intended to structure and hold a framework rather than offer tips and techniques. It allows us to reconsider work from a higher level of thinking and, from there, notice other things going on that may prove to be valuable in creating different life experiences.

In the process of moving through any kind of change, the WEL-Systems approach recognizes that change must be driven from the inside out; from inside the individual and not imposed from the outside. This approach:

- Encourages individuals to access their own internal resources for coping with change rather than relying on an outside source;
- Ensures that the communication process surrounding the change is inclusive and occurs respectfully – meaning open, direct, clear, timely and honest; and
- Engenders the belief that the larger system (work, family, community, etc.) is willing to provide the support mechanisms that will assist individuals in adjusting to the change. After all, we *are* the system.

A WEL-Systems perspective is based on some fundamental, underlying beliefs. In my own experience as an employee in large corporate systems, as well as in my experience in working with people from those systems for the last 25 years, these beliefs are unshakable and have been proven time and time again to represent the nature of being human. These beliefs are:

- Essential to the existence of an organization (or any other living system) are the people who work there. Send them home and the organization ceases to exist.

  This belief invites an awareness of an organization (or any other living system) as a nominalization; requires an exploration of the individual, leading to integration of the personal and professional, collapsing the duality of the closed-loop; and invites an exploration of the process of work itself, recognizing that all meaning is context dependent.

- People want to participate and contribute. It is the nature of being human to create, to grow and to build.

This belief encourages us to look for what's working; to seek out the positive intention that drives behavioral responses; to find what we do 'right' and invites an exploration of many of the notions that we have historically explored within a work context, with an awareness that the things we have been exploring are all nominalizations. We have been distracted by things that aren't real and that don't exist in physical space and time, allowing us to avoid what is in physical space and time: you and me. As such, this exploration lends itself to redefining some of our corporate experiences including:

Leadership – which is highly personal and involves who the leader is and not just what the leader does. As leader, my own behaviors and attitude affect and shape the people around me. As leader, am I a living expression of what I say I want from others? Am I a living model of the result that I want to produce?

Power – noticing that power and control are not the same thing. It is useful to notice when control has become its own reward. To what degree does my own uncertainty and fear of the unknown drive my need/desire for control? What distinguishes the experience of *internal* (or personal) *power* from *external power* (or power over)?

Management – as a process in perpetual motion and evolution, not as a level or a line on an org chart. Managers are facilitators, managing environments so that people can manage themselves to effectively produce a collective result. As manager, I recognize that I am powerless to control another human being.

Action – requires behavior. Do my behaviors model my intentions? Are they an example of what needs to occur in order to achieve an end? Does the cumulative effect of my actions contribute to the direction or intention I've defined?

Health – of one equals the health of the system. Each of us is a small and critical part of the larger living system, with each person being a 'cell', each division being an 'organ' in the larger living system of the corporate collective. A healthy system produces a healthy result.

Boundaries – are expected and invited rather than tolerated. Boundaries are what make creativity, innovation and health possible within living systems. Without boundaries, there is no potential for distinctions.

Beliefs/Values/Attitudes – shape reality through the perceptual filters they create and are a crucial part of any human being and therefore of any living system. To ignore them or to avoid discussion about them as a legitimate part of the business process creates artificial environments based on illusions and lies. Visible and forming part of our daily conversations, they become a fundamental part of corporate (and other) systems that are able to support and sustain life.

Power of the mind – is recognized and supported in each individual within the larger system. Thoughts are things. Everything that exists in space and time was first a thought in someone's mind. How well do I know the structures and the processes of my own mind? How consistent am I at being able to stay on the Cause side of the equation with my own thoughts? How strong are my convictions when challenged by the status quo, usually the majority?

Chapter 14

- People already know what they need in order to thrive and contribute. When provided with environments that support expression of their existing wisdom, both people and organizations blossom.

  Employees, regardless of their organizational level, are not children. In this country, we have laws that prevent that. And yet, how good are we at recognizing and honoring that people know what they need in order to be effective and make a contribution? We want others to respect this within us and yet, how willing and able are we to respect this truth in someone else, particularly when our needs are in conflict? How adept are we at creating work environments that allow for these differences to be expressed and incorporated into the way we work and ultimately, in the results we produce? How effectively do we create physical, behavioral and contextual environments that allow for open exploration of these differences? How great is our tolerance for difference, for uncertainty, for conflict?

We cannot create systems that are greater than our tolerance for uncertainty or that exceed our belief in ourselves. We cannot create systems that are more expansive than our ability to trust ourselves and each other. The greater our fear, the greater our need will be to control, and the smaller and tighter our systems will be. Inevitably, we will create systems that reflect who we are.

We cannot create systems that are greater than our tolerance for uncertainty

For more information, consider:

- *Steps to an Ecology of Mind* by Gregory Bateson
- *Thinking About Thinking* by Joseph Yeager
- *Imagineering for Health* by Serge King
- *Thought as a System* by David Bohm
- *Beliefs: Pathways to Health and Well-Being* by Robert Dilts

FULLY ALIVE

The future is uncertain…
but this uncertainty is
at the very heart of human creativity.

- Ilya Prigogine -

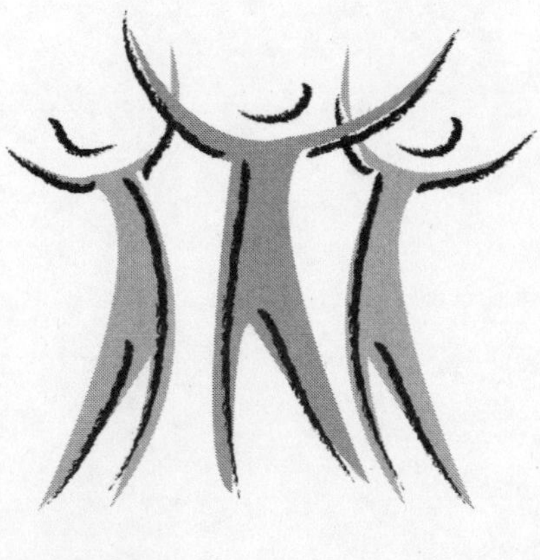

CHAPTER 6

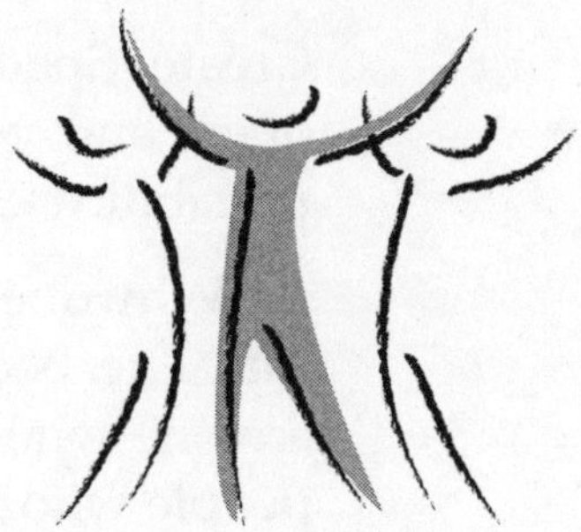

Changing It

The groundwork has been laid. What you do with the rest of your life is entirely up to you. Be mindful that every behavior has a naturally occurring consequence. Sometimes we experience that consequence as a reward; sometimes we experience it as a punishment. Whatever your experience, the naturally occurring consequences of the choices you've already made, collectively, have created the quality of your life today. How do you like it so far?

If you like what you've got and you'd like more of it, great! Just keep doing what you're doing and it will take you where you want to go. If however, you would like something else in your life, you may want to ponder the following information.

The process of change

If you remember nothing else from reading this book, remember these three words:

Space – Movement – Flow

Without Space, Movement is not possible. If you press your hands tightly together, it is impossible for anything to move between the palms of your hands.

Create Space, by allowing your hands to begin to open, and you create the invitation for Movement as a possibility. Sustained Movement results in Flow.

Why does any of this matter? Because in all the years that I've been working with people, I've yet to meet anyone who resists change. I have however, met many people who instinctively knew that they were unwilling to engage in anything that left them feeling unsafe. That's the sign of a high IQ! Creating a Space that results in people feeling safe – safe in body, mind and spirit – becomes the irresistible invitation for them to step into and engage more of themselves. If you know how to create Space in your thinking, in your language and in your behaviours, change becomes an exciting part of being alive.

Before you can change anything, you must have an awareness that you want to change. You must begin to pay attention to that part of your life experience that lends itself to the possibility of change. You may have a sense of emptiness in your life, a sense that something's missing even though you may not know what that is. Or perhaps you already have something in your life that is in some way causing you pain or no longer fills a void or keeps your attention the way it once did. Or perhaps you have a nagging sense inside you that something is calling to you and you can't quite figure out what that is.

However you define your experience, many of our clients fall into the age range of late 30's to early 50's. They experience a 'pressure' inside them that compels them to begin to seek something else in their lives. Sometimes they incorporate what they're looking for into their existing way of life – and sometimes they walk away. It takes great courage to allow ourselves to become the seeker of our own internal truth.

It takes great courage to allow ourselves to become the seeker of our own internal truth

Once we are aware of the need for change, we must be both *willing* to allow that process of change to be engaged and *able* to manage the experience of it within ourselves. We are often faced with situations where either we or the people around us 'resist' change. My belief is that people do not resist change. The desire and the need to grow and expand is the entelechy of being human – it is our natural state. That's why the pressure to take action (movement is a sign of life!) can become so intense. I do however, believe that it is a sign of intelligence not to proceed in any direction without a sense of safety.

When people *feel* safe, they are willing to step into the unknown; to try new things; and to tell the truth as they experience it inside themselves. When they do not *feel* safe, they are unwilling to let go of what they have, clinging to it for dear life as the water churns around them. An unwillingness to move forward into something new or different is not a sign of resistance; it is an indication of a lack of internal safety. Safety, or lack thereof, is always an inside job and therefore, extremely personal. If we can come to recognize and honor this as legitimate feedback in a larger process, we can engage in the kind of conversations that will result in creating a context that will allow for safety and subsequently, for movement. An unwillingness to move forward in an unsafe environment is the sign of a high IQ!

When people feel safe, they are willing to step into the unknown

An unwillingness to move forward in an unsafe environment is the sign of a high IQ!

The willingness to change

Here's a riddle for you: How many psychologists does it take to change a light bulb? The answer: One – but the light bulb must want to change.

If you do not want to change, don't waste your time and effort and energy *trying* to change because someone else thinks you should. Whether it's the boss, your parents, your spouse, your children or your guru, if you don't want to change, whatever your reason, you will not change. No one can make you or force you to think differently or do something you don't want to do. Rather than undertake such a pretense, we would be far better served to explore what it is that keeps us where we are; to notice the disadvantages and the advantages of holding to the status quo, given that all human behavior has a positive intent. You might surprise yourself.

Often times, we go through the motions because we don't want to disappoint someone or because we don't want to have to deal with the consequences of *not* going through the motions! We may even work up a sweat and look like we're really struggling to change but deep down inside, where we live, we know that nothing's going to happen because we don't want it to or we're not ready for it to happen.

We now know that all learning, all behavior and all change takes place at the level of the unconscious mind. Your unconscious mind, like everyone else's, lives deep inside you where only you can see and know what's going on. Your unconscious mind, like everyone else's, also speaks to you through the process of the body - that mind/body conduit for the transfer of information from one level of awareness to another - and is giving you sensory signals all the time. No wonder we've worked for so long and so hard to learn to ignore the sensory signals from the body! If we allowed ourselves to pay attention to them and give them credence, our lives would be forever altered.

If we allowed ourselves to pay attention to sensory signals and give them credence, our lives would be forever altered

Once you have the willingness to change, it's important that you recognize that the only thing you can change is you - *your* thoughts, *your* intentions, *your* behaviors – and *your* responses to what you experience as things outside of you. As you come more and more to trust your own internal sensory cues, change becomes a natural unfolding as opposed to an aberration in an existing structure; more like the steady, slow movement of tectonic plates than the violent upheavals of an earthquake, however small on the Richter scale.

Personal power

We also know that all change is personal and that change occurs from the inside out. The notion of power or, more specifically, personal power, is one that captures the imagination. The dictionary defines power as "the capacity to act". What we need to consider is: for what purpose? In what context? What exactly does it mean, in terms of quality of life? How do I become a person of great personal power? How would I be different from who I am now? How would my life change? And if power is a force, where does that force come from? How would I direct that force and what kind of life would I create for myself and for the people around me?

Why is it that power remains so elusive for so many? Why do we tend to think of power as something that exists outside of us, something that we can earn or simply take, maybe even buy, and then wield like a weapon? How is it that we think of power as something finite, with only so much available; that if someone else has some, we may not get enough; that power is designed to be used to make things happen, to do things to something or somebody; and if you aren't careful, someone will try to do something to you or make you do something you don't want to do. Or, worse, even take your power away! It is as if there is a shortage and we must zealously guard whatever we have for fear of it being taken or simply evaporating if we are not relentless in our vigilance.

Stripped of our sense of personal power (that is, our ability to create for ourselves a life that we want and believe to be worth living), we are left trembling

Stripped of our sense of personal power, we are left trembling in fear and uncertainty or filled with resentment and rage

in fear and uncertainty or filled with resentment and rage. We experience a deep sense of loss of dignity and a violation of our personal integrity (i.e. wholeness). If we react so profoundly to such an awareness, is it possible that personal power is a naturally occurring state and one which we hold, at some very deep level, to be our birthright?

Think about what it feels like to be at work. By the time we get to work, we've been rewarded for close to two decades for *not* thinking for ourselves but for toeing the party line, being a team player, not rocking the boat and supporting the status quo. Frequently, the ideal employee is the one who doesn't ask questions and just gets on with it; the one who doesn't talk back and the one who graciously covers your mistakes rather than drawing them to your attention.

The paradox is that if it's not right for you it will eventually not support life at the level of the larger system!

What matters is not that you create what's right for you, but that you create what's right for… the family, the business, the community, etc. The paradox is that given that larger living systems are made up of individual living systems (human beings), if it's not right for you it will eventually not support life at the level of the larger system! Because the larger system is just that – larger – it may take longer for the evidence to present itself but it will manifest over time. We are now witnessing the effects of that erosion in our existing corporate structures.

By the time we're old enough to go to work, that electrifying surge of energy, vital force or life force that once ran through our bodies seems to have cut back to a trickle. Its flow has been consistently diminished from one system to another; from the family to the church to school and finally to work. Our natural curiosity and instincts to explore – to fearlessly venture deep into unknown territory - have been replaced by rules, regulations and lengthy list of expectations. By the time we reach our early 40's, we frequently find ourselves feeling flat and lifeless; bored and wondering, 'there must be more to life than just paying the credit card bills…'; or sometimes agitated and impatient, not knowing why. Perhaps it's time we moved away from the relentless repetition of the rules and went deeper into our own awareness to rediscover our ability to not only trust but delight in the impulses that move through the body. Perhaps it's time for us to return to that place deep inside where our feelings reside and where we will discover our greatest hopes and our darkest fears.

Perhaps it's time for us to return to that place deep inside where our feelings reside - our greatest hopes and our darkest fears

We begin to notice that before life happens 'out there', it happens inside where the most private part of us lives. We begin to notice that we are quick to take ownership of the things in our lives that are working, yet reluctant to claim what's not working and quick to find someone else to blame it on. We begin to notice how easy it is for us to talk about the things we feel good about, and the degree to which we avoid conversations about the things that cause us discomfort inside. We begin to notice how easily we are distracted by the things that we can engage with ease and certainty, whether we want them or not, and how we shy away from the possibility of failing at something that we are unsure of yet know would change our lives. What if I am responsible (i.e. able to respond) for all of it – the good and the bad, the stuff that works and the stuff that makes me want to crawl back into bed and stay there!

Each of us carries deep inside of us information that is unique to us and shapes our interpretation of the world in which we live. These experiences, from conception through to our death, are wired directly into the nervous system and literally shape who we become. We already know that our core beliefs are in place by the time we're five or younger. For most of us, we rarely if ever revisit those core beliefs as structured and defined

Each of us carries deep inside of us information that is unique to us and shapes our interpretation of the world in which we live through the experiences and the wisdom of a five year old. Take a moment to consider the things that you were conditioned to believe. Do they continue to serve you? Do you feel alive, vital, dynamic and authentic? Do you like who you've become? Do you like what you've created, for yourself and others?

Our cultural conditioning has taught us to ignore the messages from the body and defer to the rules, whatever they may be, at work, at home and in relationships. We've been taught to value linguistically structured thought, which often translates to logic and reason, above all else in our lives. But have you ever noticed that before you ever think a linguistically structured thought there is always a movement of energy in the body? We experience this as the urge or intention to speak, before speech actually happens. And yet as our thoughts become more habituated, we notice the energy less and less, as it has become a habit of thought and moves through deeply rooted existing pathways, with very little resistance from tissue in the body.

We've been taught to value linguistically structured thought above all else in our lives

As you allow yourself to think new thoughts and to move away from the traditional, culturally conditioned biased thinking – to challenge the status quo, to explore new contexts – the topography of the brain is actually transformed by the action of this process and its related movement of energy. When this happens, there is a sensation that runs through the body. You have just had an original thought or a new insight; or an interpretation that is entering your awareness for the first time. It is not unusual at such times to find yourself unable to put words to what you have just experienced. When this happens, you become able to perceive your experience through new eyes; to process the data of your life through new thought models. It is now impossible for you to come to the same old conclusions.

The experiencing of an emotion or what I would call a sensory response in the body, defies accurate and/or complete expression through language, which is the tool of the intellect. Any attempt to use words to define or describe the experience to another, either through journaling or speaking/writing, fails. The map is not the territory, no matter how elaborate and detailed the map may be. Words simply cannot capture the full magnitude of the experience itself and pale in their attempts to make that experience available to another, from the outside. They must find it for themselves, inside themselves, in the truth of their *own* experience. It is the movement of that experience in the body that takes you from the level of knowledge and information to the domain of wisdom and truth. Not truth as an absolute but the truth of who you are now and who you are capable of becoming. In this context, the truth shall indeed, set you free.

The experiencing of an emotion defies accurate and/or complete expression through language

Before we can begin to acknowledge and accept the existence of emotions in the people we work/live with, we must first come to acknowledge and accept our own emotions. You can't give what you haven't got, making it impossible for you to offer an open context for hearing someone else's truth when you have neither faith in nor familiarity with your own.

You can't give what you haven't got

There is no denying the presence of an intense emotion as it moves through your body. The surge of power that snakes through the neural pathways of the flesh that makes up who you are, is impossible to ignore. In a flash of heat or cold, the wave moves through your body, carrying information and – if you're paying attention – offering insights and alternative worldviews for your consideration. If you're not paying attention, you write it off as a hot flash or a draft.

Perhaps the value of an emotional experience is simply in being fully present to it

Perhaps the value of an emotional experience is not in the story telling that follows it, nor in the logical and rational analysis that we invent to make sense of it, but in simply being fully present to it. We focus our attention on the energy as it moves, allowing it to expand fully and freely through the body. As it moves, shifting the topography of the brain, it leaves behind an altered neurology, with neurology being the vehicle for the movement of this information. It leaves behind an evolved, more expansive mechanism now available to process the next experience; and so on, and so on…

Think of blowing up a balloon. What makes a difference in the balloon isn't talking about breath; or even categorizing the different kinds of breaths one could use to blow the balloon up. What makes the difference in the balloon is actually blowing breath into it; is the *experience* of the breath itself stretching the fabric of the balloon; altering the minuscule structures that had, until now, shaped the balloon and structured it a certain way. Once breath moves through, the balloon is forever altered. It is also more receptive to the next breath and the next, and the next…..

Perhaps we all talk too much and feel too little

Being still and allowing the feelings to move completely through an open body results in the body itself being altered by the experience.[1] The body is the mechanism that 'thinks' or processes information with our intellect (linguistically structured thought) being the mechanism for describing the effects of the experience to another, after the fact. Perhaps we all talk too much and feel too little.

---

1 For more, refer to *Phoenix Rising: The Freeing of Human Potential* and Quantum TLC™.

Breathing is good!

Without breath, there is no life. Without breath, there is no wave to carry the vital force, or the life force, through the dense tissue of the body. Breathing, consciously or unconsciously, has a profound effect on how the body (the instrument that thinks) processes information.

We've already noticed that there is a direct connection between feeling and thinking. It would make great sense then, to allow what you call a feeling to move through the body and deliver its messages. As the information moves, the potential for change increases.

We've also noticed that in order for there to be movement, there must first be space. Breathing deeply into the body expands the body. We call it 'relaxing'. This expansion – inside – brings with it an environment that invites the energy to move, freely and openly, through the tissue.

If you want to be a better thinker; if you want to be smarter, let your feelings move. That does not mean that every time you have a feeling you have the right to abuse somebody with it. That will serve no one. The only value in the feeling, given that it's inside you and that there's nothing that goes on inside you that belongs to anyone but you, is in its movement inside you. Keep your hands to yourself, your lips sealed and follow these three simple suggestions:

If you want to be a better thinker; if you want to be smarter, let your feelings move

1. Breathe!

Breathing is good! We have long lost our connection to the power of our own breath. We have learned to breathe very shallowly in the chest, keeping the breath high in the body. We've discovered that when the energy moves – or the feelings come – we can stop the process by holding our breath, or by distracting ourselves with something outside of us. (Much like pulling the plug on your computer when the green light starts to blink.) But when you allow your breath to go deeper into the body, there is a corresponding opening or expansion of the body that invites movement at deeper levels of awareness. Things that you had long ago tucked far away come to life once again. You begin to notice things you've not noticed before. You can no longer ignore things that you long ago filed and often struggle to forget.

You can no longer ignore things that you long ago filed and often struggle to forget

When we begin to take breathing (which is a culturally occurring process of the body that generally occurs out of conscious awareness) and bring it into conscious awareness, it can become a powerful tool for profound change. (There are many other places where you can read about different breathing techniques and their affect on the body. Check with your local bookstore.)

Breathing deeply also allows you to access the parasympathetic nervous system response, making it impossible for you to feel fear. In such a state of internal safety, you are far better positioned to consider new things with a sense of calm and stability. As you allow breath to move through those deeper levels of the body, you will become aware of sensations in different places in your body. Pay attention to them – they have meaning.

2. Follow the impulses.

Trust your body!

Trust your body! As breath moves through your body and activates those sensory responses – or impulses - in the tissue, move your attention directly into those places and continue to breathe. Energy flows where attention goes, meaning that as you focus your attention on that place in the body, the energy of the breath will flow directly into that place, opening and expanding the tissue. This creates the space that is a pre-requisite to movement. Change requires movement.

As you breathe into these sensory responses, you may begin to notice that they move. They may begin in one area of the body and travel up or down. Go with them. Follow them from one place to the next, repeating the process as you go. As you stay with them, you'll discover that they eventually, and often quickly, dissipate.

3. Let yourself know the truth of your experience.

We have become experts at lying to ourselves and at denying ourselves our own inner awareness. Our gut feelings, our instincts about things, our vibes: all are frequently sacrificed on the altar of good manners and keeping the peace. So good have we become at this, that we even deny ourselves our own truth in the privacy of our own minds! We lie to ourselves all the time, telling ourselves that something doesn't matter when it does; that it's not important when it is; that it won't matter when we know it will. We have become experts at masking on the outside, the reflection of our internal states on the inside. Bad enough that we practice this deception with others, be they colleagues or family or friends, yet far more devastating when we practice this deception with ourselves.

We have become experts at lying to ourselves and at denying ourselves our own inner awareness

As we develop mastery at this game of self-deception and self-denial, over time we become incapable of distinguishing truth from fiction; of knowing what we really care about from what we've taught ourselves to respond to. We become enmeshed in the fabric of our own lies, living lives that, though we've created them, are not necessarily lives we want or value. With age sometimes comes the recognition of the meaninglessness of this endeavor. With age sometimes also comes the awareness of what's missing – like intimacy, with ourselves and with others.

The greatest acts of intimacy require truth: an authentic revelation of self, warts and all

The greatest acts of intimacy require truth: an authentic revelation of self, warts and all. Intimacy requires that I know myself so that I may share that with another human being. How can I give you what I don't know I have? How can I reveal to you what I have no sense of inside myself? In those rare moments when you catch a glimpse of an element of myself that even I have overlooked or hidden away, we do not move closer, we move farther apart because I do not trust the truth of your experience with me. I have no knowledge of it in myself.

We live in a world that is obsessed with sex, creating a multi-billion dollar industry in the process of our frenzied search for intimacy. We seek comfort in rubbing our bodies together with the hope that the hunger deep in the belly will be satisfied. The feast is short-lived. Like North Americanized Chinese food, you're initially stuffed from having gorged yourself on the all-you-can-eat buffet but are hungry again in a very short time.

We talk of 'making love' when people pay for sex; people who have no knowledge of each other beyond what a quick glance at the body reveals. We have even lost our capacity to make distinctions between an act of the body and an expression of the soul.

You've heard before that you can't give what you haven't got; just like you can't love someone else until you love yourself. You'll never love yourself if you can't trust your own feelings – the movement of your own life force – when it moves through your body. Perhaps, as some might suggest, those sensory responses in your body are a direct communication from what you experience as your Source. The phone's ringing; are you ready to answer it?

By the time we get to be 40, it takes great courage to tell ourselves the truth. We have invested much of our effort and energy in building work, family and community experiences that are a reflection of the things that we've said and the beliefs that we've acted upon. Sometimes, we've created systems and structures with voracious appetites for more and bigger and better; appetites that begin to devour the parts of us that are most vulnerable and least able to fend for themselves, like our fear of failing or of being inept, of not measuring up or being worthy or 'as good as' someone else. Usually, these creations involve other people – family, friends, colleagues, people in our communities – and have often become an expectation in the way they live their lives. They depend on us to maintain and perpetuate the system, since they don't know anything else. We begin to feel like we can't stop or change our minds, or just let go. Telling ourselves the truth is an act of courage; telling our truth out loud to other people is an act of transformation.

We've created systems and structures with voracious appetites that begin to devour the parts of us that are most vulnerable and least able to fend for themselves

Telling ourselves the truth is an act of courage; telling our truth out loud to other people is an act of transformation

Imagine what work/life could become if we told the truth – first, inside ourselves and then to each other. Imagine if we were both willing and able to tell our truth about ourselves, losing interest in telling our truth about someone else. No more pretending, no more politicking, no more doing things we don't believe in. Imagine if work became an authentic, consistent extension of life. Imagine if our work environments offered an experience where we felt safe in telling the truth of our individual experience, not because work had changed but because we had changed. And imagine that the truth of that experience, even when uncomfortable, was invited because of the contribution that it could make to each of us and to the larger whole? Imagine if I told myself the truth inside me, about work. Would they want me? Could I/would I still go there? Or would I move on?

We were born knowing the truth of what we needed; we were trained out of it along the way, in the name of politesse and social acceptance. We've even named that time in life – the terrible twos – when we first begin to be chastised for saying what's on our minds. Truth-telling (inside and out) is a naturally occurring process in human beings as evidenced by a child's tendency to say out loud what's rolling around inside them. We are the ones who've made knowing and speaking the truth an aberration, through cultural conditioning at all levels of the system. Then, we spend years of our adult lives in therapy trying to get it back. Go figure!

We are the ones who've made knowing and speaking the truth an aberration

Sixty seconds of authentic presence will undo decades of habituated thinking. This is why authenticity is so dangerous to the status quo.

If you did nothing other than these three things, your life would change profoundly. Don't take my word for it – try it yourself. The next time you're in a meeting, sit back; take some deep breaths and relax your body; let it open and keep it open through these deep breaths. Let yourself notice the discrepancy between the things you say inside yourself and the things you say out loud. Notice what happens inside your body when the words you say out loud don't match the way you feel inside. You might as well begin to notice – everyone else does. They may not necessarily be able to tell you what they've picked up on; they just have a 'sense' (a body response) about it and pull away. The things we make up are often far worse than any truth we could tell or be told.

We like to think that our actions and words are dictated by our intellects and our rational, linear, logical thinking self. And yet, if you were to pay attention, you might begin to notice that the body response always comes first. Then, after this energy has moved through, we find a way to rationalize the legitimacy of that body response using logic and analysis to make it acceptable. It is no longer acceptable for us to want something just because we want it. We have to have a good reason for it or at least deserve it; or have worked hard for it or earned it. Sometimes, we just want it because we want it – period.

It is no longer acceptable for us to want something just because we want it

The context for change: natural rhythms and instincts

Before we can get to where we want to go, we must be willing to leave where we are. Every journey begins with the first step. In this journey, the first step is willingness (desire or intention) and the second is ability (skills or tools). In order to create something other than what we already have, we must be both willing and able to do so.

Willingness is an internal state; a state of being that is expressed from the inside out. It is driven by our internal context, or world-view, and includes our tolerance for failure and our capacity for delighting in the adventure of not knowing. In this particular journey, there are three critical requirements:

- A willingness to acknowledge that what we're doing right now isn't producing the results we say we want.

  Imagine yourself witnessing a conversation between two people who do not speak the same language. You may notice one person speaks and when the other person looks puzzled or uncertain or when he/she begins to respond in their language, you watch the first person begin to speak faster or more intensely, or even louder! In the end, both parties walk away, with nothing having changed.

Continuing to do what we already know how to do – not because it works but because it's familiar and gives us the illusion of taking action - only doing it faster or harder or louder, isn't going to change anything for us, either. An awareness of this can put us in a frightening situation since we are trained to always know and have an answer; to rely on our analysis and our intellects to provide those answers; and never to take action unless we're certain of the outcome. This may work well in the Newtonian world of Environment and Behavior. But in the quantum biological world of human beings, whether at work, at home or in the larger community and at those higher levels of thinking, analysis and logic will not get you where you want to go.

We must be willing to recognize that when the horse dies, get off! We may not know what to do instead but we sure know that continuing to do what we're already doing isn't going to get us to where we want to go.

- A willingness to be curious about the thinking behind the behaviors/results of others.

In order to live this, we must let go of our judgment and/or interpretation that there is something wrong with what's already there; that the result that we are already getting is somehow an indication of something being broken or deficient. A genuine state of curiosity would require recognition that what's happening right now is live, moment-to-moment information on the current result. Getting curious about this rather than trying to get rid of it will allow us to notice the popcorn trail that leads back to the higher-level structures of thinking that created the result in the first place. You already know by now that when you create a shift at a higher level of thinking, everything below it changes all by itself. Magic!

- A willingness to be wrong or to not have an answer, creating an opportunity to be able to do something differently – or to ask bigger questions!

In a dualistic or polarized culture, such as the one we've grown up in and continue to perpetuate in our larger living systems, being wrong is not a good thing! Being wrong frequently has consequences attached to it that are in some way painful or, at least, uncomfortable. However, if we want something other than what we currently have and if we want something that is greater than incremental change, we must be willing to step into the domain of what we don't even know we don't know (Figure 1).

We must go in here, unarmed and without a map, and be willing to navigate through this uncharted territory. This vast area of the unknown is the very stuff of creativity. Imagine who we could become if we were to regain our delight in the unpredictable and our sense of playfulness about and acceptance of our own and each other's foibles. After all, calling an experience a 'mistake' has been an acquired skill. There was once a time when we called it living, and felt it to be an adventure!

Calling an experience a 'mistake' has been an acquired skill. There was once a time when we called it living, and felt it to be an adventure!

Chapter 6

The Ability: Tools of the Trade

Once there is a willingness to move forward, it helps to have tools that will not only do what needs to be done but will do the job in a way that allows for wholeness – or integrity – of the entire experience. Remember that old saying: when you only have a hammer, you think everything is a nail? Same idea. In a WEL-Systems context, having the tool is only the first step; how you use that tool (with a gentle tap or a heavy hand) will be guided by the degree to which you recognize and honor the naturally occurring wisdom in yourself and in the people around you.

To paraphrase Einstein once again, the problems of today cannot be resolved at the same level of thinking that created them. If you want to raise your thinking to a level that is higher than the level of thinking that created the 'problem', you're going to need tools that are different from the ones you're already using; the ones that come under the flag of 'the tried and true'. After all, 'tried and true' is what got you here! You're going to have to step back and re-assess your definition of the 'problem' and consider that the tools you need have always been there – you've just never noticed them before.

A WEL-Systems context for change – personal, professional or organizational – is a huge context that allows for recognition of what's already there. Like the world was always round and it just took a while for someone to notice, the tools we need to create a more expansive experience have always been there. Inside you and inside me. We've just never noticed them before, or considered them to be of any value.

We've already explored how there are only two things going on in the world: the conversation you have with yourself and the subsequent conversation you have with another human being, be that at home, at work or in the community. We've also explored how you can't change the conversation you have with another human being unless and until you are able to change the conversation you are having with yourself, first. All other conversations are driven by that first conversation – either as the speaker and how I determine what I'll say; or as the listener, and how I interpret what I hear - since it is this conversation that drives the structure of our universe. If we are going to change anything in our world, we must first discover a consistent and predictable way to influence that first conversation, and the inside thinking processes of an individual human being.

We need a tool or tools that will allow us to raise our thinking to those higher levels that will take us beyond the content of the problem. We need tools that will allow us to go beyond the content level (i.e. where, when and what) and allow us to consider those bigger, more expansive questions (i.e., how, why, which, who, who else) that will invite consideration of the process or the structure of human behavior. That takes us back to the brownie recipe.

We need a tool or tools that will allow us to raise our thinking to those higher levels that will take us beyond the content of the problem

The content of human behavior is the brownie itself. With nuts or without, when we talk about the content of the brownies we are talking about the end result that comes out of the oven. It's already a done deal. The same principle applies to human behavior. By the time you're telling the story about the behavior (I said, then you said, then I did…), it's already a done deal. If you want to change it, you have to go before the experience of it and notice what it is a reflection of. Like the brownies are a reflection of the recipe, so the behavior is a reflection of its strategy. To change the quality of our lives – at work or at home or elsewhere – we must first change the things we say and do that result in the unfolding of our experience. To change the things we say and do, we must first understand the recipe – or the strategy and structure – that makes these intelligent choices for us, so that we may choose differently the next time.

The most effective tool that we know of for addressing the structure of human behavior is NLP (Neuro Linguistic Programming) in a WEL-Systems context[2]. NLP has evolved over the last 25 years or so and has become much greater than the sum of its parts. Throughout the years, numerous books have been written on NLP with much attention focused on the techniques of NLP that allow for rapid change. A trip to your local bookstore will entice you with books on NLP applied to a variety of topics including sales, leadership, health, training and management. Because NLP lends itself to addressing the structure of human behavior rather than the content, its potential is unlimited in its usefulness in any area of human expression.

As a tool for change, NLP can be taught and applied in either a closed-loop or an open-loop system. When applied in a closed-loop system, it can be experienced as manipulative, abusive, harsh and controlling. When engaged in a WEL-Systems context, it is experienced as expansive, inviting and safe. In an open-loop application, NLP is an invitation to bring to conscious awareness naturally occurring phenomena of the human body. In a closed-loop application, it is a technique to be applied to a problem; or a pattern to be run on someone or something to be done to someone else. In an open-loop experience, the practitioner takes direction from the client. In a closed-loop experience, the practitioner knows best.

---

2 Refer to Appendix for an extensive exploration of NLP in a WEL-Systems context. "NLP: Yesterday, Today and Tomorrow" demonstrates NLP to be an owner's manual for naturally occurring functions of the human body.

An open-loop application requires an awareness that NLP is not the context for change, it is the tool. The larger context of the WEL-Systems approach draws on the natural wisdom of the body with NLP as a way of creating the safety that is essential to a vital opening; of allowing the inside to surface in what I do/say outside. WEL-Systems creates the space; NLP allows for acceleration of the movement.

Over the years, NLP has evolved from the original work of John Grinder and Richard Bandler into a significant body of knowledge that can be found in other ways in all areas of human expression. This would make sense since the original work had its origins in the observations of the naturally occurring behaviors of people who were very effective in their particular area of expertise (i.e. Milton Erickson and Virginia Satir, to name a couple). In the last 25 years, significant contributions have been made through the shared experiences of others who have brought their observations to the field, as well. As we grow and expand as human beings, so the field of NLP reflects that growth and expansion while at the same time feeding back into it - an example of the power of NLP in an open-loop system.

In our work with NLP in the last ten years, we have been shown, time and time again, that NLP is a naturally-occurring phenomenon of the human nervous system and, as such, we are all natural experts at its expression. In a world that has for decades been focused on the intellect and the process of the conscious mind, NLP has helped us to notice the power of the process of the body and its natural wisdom. NLP will often allow for the evidence that the conscious mind requires in order for there to be enough safety to engage the process of the unconscious mind, or the body.

We labor under the false illusion that we are very private and personal beings. And yet, with every word we say, every judgment we make and every behavior we manifest, we are revealing the inside of us to the rest of the world. NLP is a practical and useful tool for not only recognizing these expressions but for being better able to understand and appreciate – or get curious about – the underlying structure or recipe that produced these words/actions to begin with. With this approach, safety is maintained and movement is accelerated.

NLP is a science of human behavior that allows us – finally! – to return to trusting that we see what we see, we hear what we hear and we know what we know. An awareness of the information of NLP gives us permission, once again, to trust our instincts about things and to allow ourselves to know our own truth and to be able to recognize someone else's. The potential defies description.

Characteristics of a WEL-Systems® approach to change

A WEL-Systems approach is one that consciously, mindfully and purposefully engages a high-level of thinking and seeks intentionally to create a context that invites intention and direction (higher levels of thinking) rather than specifics (low levels of thinking). Remembering that the problems of today cannot be resolved at the same level of thinking that created them, it is an approach that creates a context for exploring and addressing the 'problem' that is larger than the problem itself.

A WEL-Systems context for change has some guideposts or markers to help you pay attention to what you are creating. These markers are part of the feedback process of the system itself to help you determine if the WEL-Systems context itself is a living model of that which it supports. Here's what to watch for.

A WEL-Systems context:

- Is an open-loop system (see *Figure 3*) with all the characteristics of an open-loop.
- Recognizes that the health of the individual equals the health of the larger system. This requires recognition that work is personal, and that people need to rest, relax and play. They also need time to themselves to regenerate and the space to structure routines that support their natural rhythms.
- Respects that boundaries are to be expected and encouraged, and not just tolerated as a nuisance to the corporate process. Honoring the process of boundaries also honors the process of saying 'no' – and recognizes that sometimes you will need/want to say no, and sometimes someone else will say no to you. It is equally valid both ways.
- Acknowledges the value inherent in the exiting situation or experience, as it is. What we have now is a natural progression of what we've been evolving into. No point in blaming or shooting the messenger; nor is there any value in investing ourselves in the coulda/shoulda/woulda game. There is recognition that the quality of our lives is not dependent on the accuracy of our answers but on the courage of our questions. What are the questions that we need to be asking, of ourselves and others, that will allow us to build what we want from where we are now?
- Legitimizes and validates a world view that beliefs, values and attitudes are an authentic part of the business process and are discussed openly and clearly. Our work environments today are permeated with nominalizations – those words that are shorthand

Beliefs, values and attitudes are an authentic part of the business process for the philosophy or intention they represent. The more we move away from the specifics of that which exists in space and time – those things that can be validated with external sensing - the more we are required to draw on nominalizations. The greater our intention or goal, the more we will be required to draw on nominalizations to allow for the expanse of that intention. And yet, if we do not take the time to share information with each other on the very personal meaning of these nominalizations, we inadvertently find ourselves working at cross-purposes. No malice of intent – just a lack of information. This requires that we begin to bring back into alignment or wholeness – or integrity – the dualities of the personal and the professional; the private and the public; the subjective and the objective; and the inside and the outside of who we are as individual human beings.

- Recognizes that control or power over things/people/events/environments has become synonymous with our current notions of leadership or management. In a parent/child model, this approach is not only tolerated (sometimes grudgingly and with sniper attacks) but also welcomed for its caretaking. (I'll do what you want me to do as long as you take care of me.) In a WEL-Systems™ context, there is a recognition that adults are able to take responsibility for themselves; and that personal power, or a sense of knowing and being able to manage our own internal states, is a far more empowering and productive experience. From this place of internal or personal power, you can trust that 'yes' means 'yes' and not 'I'll go along because I have to but don't turn your back...' There is meaning to someone giving you their word.

- Recognizes, supports and encourages expansion of the power of the mind. This means acknowledging that as the individual expands his/her ability to process information that moves inside them, they become more able to bring the benefits of this experience into the work place. As the larger system of the organization contributes to this expansion by providing time, resources and opportunities for it to be engaged and enhanced, the individuals who benefit from this experience also become more willing to share these benefits with the company; and will *feel* respected, validated and appreciated. It's personal.
- Acknowledges and values that the process of the open-loop system is the feedback mechanism. That opening and closing; that on-going, never-ending rhythmic cycle of movement is the mechanism that allows for the space within which the movement will take place: movement of information, of attitudes, of people, of events. The need to control that is assuaged by the effort to make things predictable – to stay the same – is replaced with a comfortable awareness of the ebb and flow of information, along with the accompanying signals and messages. The canaries in the mines are witnessed and heard.
- Holds that finally, the power of the system is in the context, not in any particular application of its principles. The larger the context you can continue to create, the greater the opportunity you can invite into your day-to-day experience. A WEL-Systems® context draws on the power of thought, combined with the power of conscious choice, and holds the potential for taking any 'problem' into those higher levels of thinking for 'resolution'.

Consider, for a moment, some of the 'problems' that you've been experiencing either at work or home or anywhere else for that matter. Perhaps those 'problems' are even occurring deep inside you. Take that problem, as you currently define it; give yourself permission – just for this exercise – to engage the three basic requirements for movement; and run the problem through the levels of thinking. You may be pleasantly surprised by the things you notice.

For more information, consider:

- *Phoenix Rising: The Freeing of Human Potential* by Louise LeBrun
- *Love and Power: Awakening to Mastery* by Lynn Andrews
- *Trances People Live* by Stephen Wolinsky
- *NLP: The New Psychology of Personal Excellence* by Seymour and O'Connor
- *Mastering the Hidden Self* by Serge King
- *Bridging Science and Spirit* by Norman Friedman
- *Tree of Dreams: A Spirit Woman's Vision of Transition and Change* by Lynn Andrews
- *Finite and Infinite Games* by James Carse
- *When the Horse Dies, Get Off... And Stop Dragging It Around!* by Louise LeBrun

FULLY ALIVE

Until one is committed
There is hesitancy, the chance to draw back,
Always ineffectiveness.

Concerning all acts of initiative (and creation)
There is one elementary truth,
The ignorance of which kills countless ideas
And splendid plans:
That the moment one definitely commits oneself,
Then Providence moves too.
All sorts of things occur to help one
That would otherwise never have occurred.

A whole stream of events issues from the decision,
Raising in one's favor all manner
Of unforeseen incidents and meetings
And material assistance,
Which no man could have dreamt
Would have come his way.

W.N. Murray
The Scottish Himalayan
Expedition – 1951

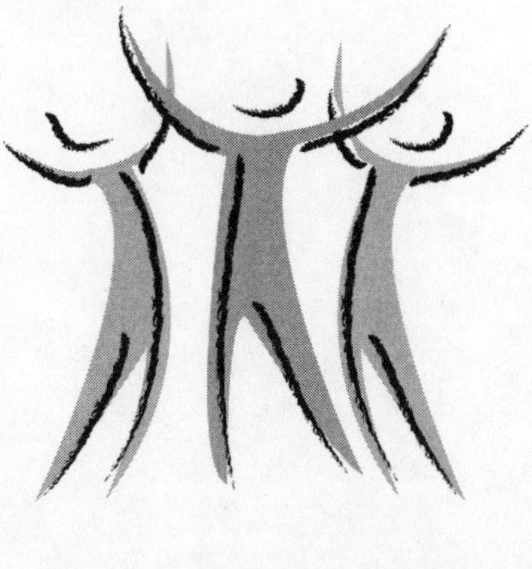

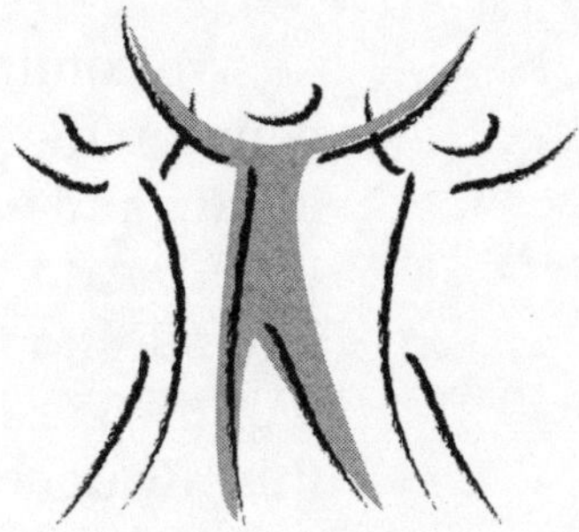

CHAPTER 7

The Future Unfolds

If you grew up in North America, you likely are held in the vice grip of the industrial-age view of work. Since as far back as 1925, science has been challenging our 'traditional' worldview, with much of that information spilling over from the laboratories into our living rooms. Even with all that information, we continue to dichotomize the personal and the professional, the private and the public and though we may have begun to apply this new information to our personal lives, we continue to structure Newtonian organizations in a quantum age.

Even though the information of the New Science has entered our consciousness through some of the more popularized books and audio/television programs, we continue to separate our personal expansion from our work environments, hiding away who we have become when we walk through the doors to the office/plant/shop/store. We somehow continue to think that we are the odd one out; that we're weird; and that other people won't understand. (A recent marketing survey in the U.S. indicates that one in every four Americans supports 'New Age' thinking. These numbers represent a massive economic force in the culture.) We continue to proceed in our work environments as if we didn't know these things and as if the people we work with can't handle this information. We're wrong.

We continue to be baffled by how to bridge the gap between the potential and the possibility that the science invites and what we've called the practicality of the 'real' world. And yet, this same science challenges and calls into question the very structure and validity of this 'real' world. We continue to go about our daily living with this awareness pressing itself into our lives while we pretend that it's not there; that things are the way they always have been; and that we, as human beings, are small, struggling and too inept to live the potential of what we've come to discover.

I am often amused by the frequency with which people tell me that they understand this information; that they recognize its power; and they can appreciate this New Science, but they are convinced that the people they work and live with would not be able to. I have actually had the opportunity to work with a group of executives with each, privately, saying this very thing about the other. Who's limiting who?

The plan is... there is no plan!

When you live life at the lower levels of thinking, it is very easy to come up with the details. That's what those levels are all about: where, when and what. But when you move your thinking to higher levels, the information that is readily substantiated by external sensing begins to disappear, leaving only big questions that lead to bigger questions. The paradox is that in the asking of the big question, the answer has already moved through the body, allowing for the next big question. It has often been said that if you can come up with the question, you already have the answer.

At those higher levels, there is less attention on detail than there is on intention and direction. It has been said that 'energy flows where attention goes'. If energy is akin to the force that allows for movement, then that force will naturally be directed to whatever you focus your attention on. If you focus your attention at low levels of thinking, that's where and what you'll create. If you move your attention up to higher levels, then the energy flow will shift to allow for creation at those levels to unfold.

Here's the good news: anything's possible. Here's the bad: it's up to you to write the recipe. If you want something that works for you, whether you're the boss or the leader or the colleague or the parent, it has to come from you. What we are in the habit of doing is taking things that come from other people who have invested their time and their attention, and then overlaying that on what we have. We are not they. Our problems are not their problems. The uniqueness of you/your situation/your experience will not be resolved by settling for someone else's solutions. It has been said that in life, you don't get what you deserve – you get what you settle for. You must produce your own results if you want it to work.

Here's the good news: anything's possible. Here's the bad: it's up to you to write the recipe

The solution will surface in the questions. In your team (whether your 'team' is on the playing field or at the board room or the kitchen table), the solutions to your problems will surface when you talk to each other; explore those nominalizations that you've all taken for granted; take responsibility for yourselves; notice how you've been a part of the problem and how you can become a part of the solution; stop blaming each other; and tell the truth. In your boardroom, your solutions will surface when you do exactly the same thing; and when you stop trashing 'the leader' and start looking for how you can create for yourself what you say you need from someone else; call up from inside yourself the things you experience as deficiencies in others.

The solution will surface in the questions

The traditional 'training' programs that we have legitimized at work – by paying for them and making work time available to engage them – have been low-level thinking kinds of programs. They have been content driven and technique based. They have had and will continue to have their place and they are neither appropriate to nor effective in resolving the far greater challenge in our work experience. We are at a point in our own evolution where we must redefine the experience of work, itself!

An individual undergoing expansion will naturally bring expansion to the organization: healthier individual systems build healthier organizational systems

Higher level thinking programs are context driven; process specific; and are directed at the expansion of the individual as an individual and not as the role they occupy in the organization. An individual undergoing expansion will naturally bring expansion to the organization: healthier individual systems build healthier organizational systems.

Our 'traditional' training is not working; it's not getting us where we say we want to go. In order to maintain some kind of alignment, either we have to change the kind of programming we offer or we have to change what we say we want. One way or the other, it's time to stop the crazy-making effects of saying one thing and doing another. We need to move away from 'training' and move into 'education'. Training is tactical (low level thinking); education is strategic. We need to stop teaching people what to think and start teaching them about *how* they think; and how to think differently, by choice.

We need to stop teaching people what to think and start teaching them about how they think

Getting personal

Often, whether in public programs or in-house delivery, the questions is asked: how do I make a difference here? Where do I start? How can I get my manager/supervisor/president/mother/husband/sibling to understand this and change? My response is always the same.

For all you Star Trek fans, think of the holodeck. For those of you who are out of this loop, on the good ship Enterprise, there is a room that is referred to as the holodeck. To the uninitiated, this is a seemingly empty room, with grid lines running its length and width. Prior to entering the room, you would have a chat with the computer and you tell the computer what you want to experience, like: you want to be in the Swiss Alps, skiing; with this particular temperature and these specific snow conditions; surrounded by these types of people, with this food and wine; at this particular time of day. The green light on the computer blinks, and within seconds the computer responds that your program is ready. You push the button, the doors open and you step onto the holodeck.

And there you are – in the Swiss Alps, just as you ordered, with everything as you have requested it, right down to the cheese. You can ski on the snow, eat the food, drink the wine, and interact with the people. It's as if all of it were real, with the only distinguishing feature being your awareness that you created it all. The only thing on the holodeck that is 'real' is you; everything else is a holographic projection.

As you go about enjoying your experience, you get a call from the Bridge of the Enterprise. You command the computer to freeze the program. Everything around you – except you – freezes; stops; becomes motionless. When you discover you are wanted on the Bridge immediately, you command the computer to end the program. In a matter of seconds, all disappears but you and the room with the grid lines.

Imagine for a moment that life is a holographic projection. There is actually science that suggests that we do indeed, live in a holographic universe. If that is so, and our lives are actually holographic projections of our construction (from the inside) to our experience (of the outside); and that the only thing 'real' in your hologram is you, what point is there in judging and blaming anyone in your holographic experience? After all, you did create the experience to your own specifications. Not only that, what point is there in judging and blaming something that isn't really there?

How much of our 'real' life experience is actually an invention of our own minds? A reflection of the structures of our own Iceberg of the Self™ as applied to our observations of others? How much of what we experience do we actually pre-determine by our expectations and our own limitations of understanding? Perhaps the expression "you create your own reality" goes far deeper than we know.

Making a difference

If you want your life to change, at work or elsewhere, start with you

If you want your life to change, at work or elsewhere, start with you. Start with that conversation that goes on inside of you, the one that determines everything else that you say and do, and eventually express outside of you. Start by telling yourself the truth, as you know it to be for you, and by allowing that truth to come to light inside you. That you never tell another soul is entirely up to you. It isn't saying it out loud that will make the difference; it's saying it out loud, inside, so that you'll know. Once this information moves through the system that you are, the neurology changes and so does the way you experience the world.

Start with you - not as an employee or a parent or a spouse but as a human being. What are you afraid of? What keeps you where you are? Why do you keep doing the things that you do? What prevents you from doing something different? Who do you usually blame for the state of your life? What side of the cause/effect equation of life do you stand on? How did you learn that? Where did you learn right from wrong? Where else did you learn what you know; and when was the last time you pondered it, or held it up for scrutiny in the light of your current awareness?

Get curious about how you got to be who you are. How long have you felt like a victim? When did it start? What choices have you made along the way that have perpetuated your experience? What part have you played in the unfolding of your own dilemma? Who would you have to become to build a different life for yourself? What stops you from doing it now? How much of the parent/child model drives your behaviors? Where did you learn your attitudes and outlook on what you experience as authority? What's familiar about your current situation; and where have you had this experience before?

The bottom line to any change is you – not as an employee, or a spouse, or a member of the community - but you, as an individual human being. Once you begin to take responsibility for what goes on inside of you, the results of that will begin to appear in everything you touch. Change inside first; it reflects outside.

Change inside first; it reflects outside

Strategies for change

Some time ago, Dr. Bruce Lipton was being interviewed on a national radio show. He said that he used to go around the country telling people that they are in charge of their lives. His science had proven to him, beyond a shadow of a doubt, that this was indeed the case. But he added that, based on people's reactions to this statement, he now goes around the country telling people that they are in charge of their lives *once they know that they can be* in charge of their lives. In other words, before you can take action you have to be conscious enough to know that taking action exists as a possibility for you.

If you want to significantly and profoundly affect the quality of your life, wherever you happen to be living it, get conscious! Getting conscious requires that you become mindful and that you begin to 'pay attention' to the process of choice; noticing that you are indeed choosing. Here are some thoughts on getting conscious:

- Begin by paying attention to what goes on around you and notice that you are the system. There's nothing 'out there' that is separate from you. Your thoughts and the subsequent inner or emotional states are structures of your own creation. The good news is that it means you're in charge! If you had the power to create it in the first place, you now hold the power to change it.

If you had the power to create it in the first place, you now hold the power to change it

- Start with the conversation that goes on inside you. Listen for it. Notice how you talk to yourself about yourself now; about your potential. Listen inside to have revealed to you your views about the world; about other people; about your ability to function in that world; about what you can achieve and what you'll never have. Begin to ask for this information; to seek it out with intention and then pay attention to what begins to surface.
- Notice that you can raise your thinking to higher levels simply by choosing to do so and by asking yourself the questions that are tied to that level of thinking. Begin to ask big questions, like: who am I capable of becoming? (Identity); who have I been culturally conditioned to believe that I am?(Beliefs/Values/Attitudes)?; who else and what else matters

to me in my life; how am I connected to them now; and how do I want to be connected in the future? (Spirituality).

- Pick up a book! (Note the suggested reading at the end of the chapters or visit our website for suggestions.) Explore some of the more popular literature on what's referred to as the 'New Science', and its practical application to the way you live your life from one day to the next. Begin to step into 'what you don't know you don't know' and allow your curiosity to be your guide. Allow your primary perceptual filter of space/time/matter/energy to be shaken up a bit by the information that comes from a quantum perspective. Given that this filter is a primary filter for the structure of reality, you may notice your particles accelerating!

- Take a course, attend a seminar or take the plunge into those things that you've often dismissed or ridiculed. Let yourself browse through the things your cynicism has prevented you from looking at, until now. Let your skepticism be your guide, acting like radar to draw you toward those areas for further exploration. It doesn't have to cost a lot of money in order for it to be valuable and practical. You can learn much from books and audio tapes that will make it possible for you to begin to change your life now, without the guidance and assistance of a 'guru'.

Let yourself browse through the things your cynicism has prevented you from looking at

- Listen to audio products, at home or in the privacy of your car; with a headset while you're running or walking; at your convenience and for as long as you choose. If you find yourself hearing things you don't like, ask yourself what's going on inside you. Is the material not useful to you or is it that you're bumping up against a belief that you are not willing or able to challenge?

- Explore some of the latest thinking from science about yourself as a human being. Don't rely on the stuff (a technical term) you were taught in high school. If you were born before 1985, you're already out of date, and out of touch with what we now suspect is 'reality'.
- Give yourself permission to call time out, to take a break, to be able to read and listen and participate without having to make any quick changes. Let things wash over you; take your time; listen to your body; and allow yourself the luxury of pondering. Sit still; spend time alone; and listen to your own thoughts.
- Rediscover the things that you like to do; that make you laugh; that are a way for you to play. Relax. Slow down the pace of your speech; speak deliberately; and take the time to ponder before you respond. Giving yourself that 30-second interlude will help you notice how frequently you respond to things out of habit and are often unaware of what you're saying.

Notice how frequently you respond to things out of habit

- Remember that breathing is good! Begin to bring the idea of The Iceberg of the Self™ into your meetings. Take the time to educate and inform the people you spend time with. If they knew what you knew, believed what you believe and felt like you feel, they'd do what you do. Never attribute to malice that which can be attributed to mindlessness.

Never attribute to malice that which can be attributed to mindlessness

- Explore your beliefs about what a boss is, what a manager is and what a leader is. Notice how much of your business structures require being in control and notice what it feels like inside when you think you aren't in control. Discover your underlying beliefs about people – especially employees that report to you. What do you need to watch for? What can you trust? What can't you rely on?

- If you're not 'the boss' (keeping in mind that you're only the boss until you talk to the person that you report to, and that everyone is accountable to somebody, somewhere), notice how much of your thinking about 'the boss' comes from that parent/child model. Where did you learn about authority? What does authority represent to you? What is the relationship between authority and control? How different are you at work from who you are at home? And remember, given how we are always revealing ourselves, if you think that your boss is the part of the horse that's over the fence last, he/she knows it!
- Dare to dream the big dreams of who you are capable of becoming; of the life that you are capable of creating for yourself and the people you touch. Never mind what other people have to say about what you should be permitted; or what you deserve. Remember, other people's opinions are about them, not you.
- THINK FOR YOURSELF! Let yourself question and challenge the things that don't feel right, look right or sound right to you; or make sense to you – even if at first, you only do that inside yourself. Give yourself the time and opportunity to strengthen that first conversation (the one that goes on inside yourself) before you dive into the one that goes on outside. The one that goes on outside is heavily guarded and supported by collective thought. Expect it to bite back when you poke at it and that way, you won't be surprised or derailed when it does!

Expect it to bite back when you poke at it

Collapsing dualities

How much longer can we continue to split ourselves down the middle and expect to stay well – as an individual, as a family, as a community, as an organization, as a planet? How much longer can we continue to say one thing and do something else? How much more evidence do we need that things aren't working; that what we're doing isn't going to get us to where we say we want to go? How much longer before we begin to notice that there isn't anything going on – at work or anywhere else – that we haven't created? And what is it going to take for us to notice that if we can create this, we can create anything? The bigger question is: what do we want?

In order for us to begin to regain a sense of alignment, a sense of wholeness or integration, we could start by noticing and collapsing certain polarizations or dualities that have permeated the culture for at least several generations now. That it has been that way does not mean that it's the way it should be, or even that it's the best way for it to be. It simply means that habit has run its natural course. Is it useful for us to keep doing that?

Most of us have been raised in the land of right and wrong; good and bad; black and white. It is a binary system that has allowed for a certain degree of simplicity and the illusion of control by taking highly complex situations (and people) and reducing them to the lowest common denominator and then making a judgment about it. For a long time, the vast majority of us have been willing to be squeezed into a little, tiny space that, although suffocating, has to some degree allowed us to feel protected. But we must be growing up because what once felt like protection is now beginning to feel like confinement.

The vast majority of us have been willing to be squeezed into a little, tiny space

Much of what we have been, and continue to be, trained into relies heavily on the process of the intellect at the cost of the process of the body. Our need for logical, rational and linear thinking has resulted in our having to deny the truth of the experience in the body. We have for generations separated the process of the intellect (or the conscious mind) from the process of the body (the unconscious mind) to the extent that many of us have come to experience the body process, or the unconscious mind, as the enemy. This part of us communicates through intuition, gut feel, a 'sense' about something, instinct; much of which historically has been dismissed as illogical and irrelevant.

To bring the process of the conscious mind back into alignment with the process of the unconscious mind; allowing each to do what it is designed to do and does best; and accessing the combined power of the two re-united, would also bring a stabilizing force into our experience of being human. Once the initial distrust, one of the other, has been bridged, that sense of alignment allows for the certainty to stand in our own truth.

When we can collapse back into one compelling force, the dualities - of the conscious and the unconscious mind; the private and the public; the personal and the professional; the inside and the outside; and the illusion of self and other - we can begin to bring a sense of life and vitality back into our work experience; to bring the whole self into the work effort; and to bring the full commitment and energy of alignment back into our intention of contribution to self, other and community. And what is work if not a group of individuals, coming together to produce a particular result? When did we start calling it 'work' and separate it from 'life'?

When did we start calling it 'work' and separate it from 'life'?

What you do with your life is up to you. What you do with this material when you go back to work is up to you. You can continue to have work be outside you – in which case you will find yourself on the effect side of the equation – or you can take some time to consider the possibility that your experience of work is one that you created, whether you like it or not. You may not yet know how you want to change that experience, but at least now, you know you can. From here on in, it's a choice.

Your experience of work is one that you created, whether you like it or not

Pay attention to what you want to become – the direction you want to go in - and choose consciously and in alignment with that intention. Let the potential of who you are capable of becoming pull you into the future, one choice at a time; and then the next, and the next… Take the time to discover who you want to become; where you want to be; and how you want to connect with life as it unfolds around you. If you don't, you'll have no sense of a goal or an intention. And if you don't choose for yourself, you'll end up as a bit player in the manifestation of someone else's dream. If you don't choose, someone else will choose for you.

If you don't choose for yourself, you'll end up as a bit player in the manifestation of someone else's dream

An invitation

Each of us carries within the seed of our own greatness: the magnificence of who we are and the potential of who we are to become. This expressive, creative force inside us is like a growing fetus, developing and waiting to be born. Over time, this force grows and expands inside of us, moving from a potential life force to one that will become self-sustaining. At one point, it must be released. Held hostage in the body by fear of its birth, it will die - and we will die with it.

Allow yourself to remember what happens in life when we consistently and relentlessly silence our own expression. For a while, it continues to grow, pushing up against our own resistance. But eventually, over time, it ceases to move and grow, and it stops. As the life force drains from the truth of who we are, so does our passion for life; our capacity for joy, delight and playfulness; and our hope and trust in the future.

Only I can give birth to my own potential

Only I can give birth to my own potential. The expanse of who I am to become resides in me – not outside of me – and can only be freed by me.

We each carry within us the expansive, expressive powerful self. It is through hearing ourselves and trusting in what is revealed; allowing it to flow from its creation in our bellies, up through our bodies, fired by the passion of our solar plexus and tempered by the compassion of the heart, that it makes its way to our throat – the gateway to sound and the platform for self-expression. In its richness and readiness to be known, we must release the flow from between our lips and reveal the sounds of our authentic choice into the external world. In so doing, the birth is complete.

The spirit of who we are has been set free and taken shape in the sounds of our own voice. The expression of our thoughts, the evidence of our choosing and the effects we produce are there to be witnessed in the Universe, freeing up the space to create again.

Raising the bar just a little higher, consider the following:

- *The Power Deck* by Lynn Andrews
- *Manifest Your Destiny* by Wayne Dyer
- *An Inconvenient Truth* by Al Gore
- *Ramtha: The White Book*
- *The Nature of Personal Reality: A Seth Book* by Jane Roberts
- *The Nature of the Psyche: A Seth Book* by Jane Roberts
- *The Chaos Point: The World at the Crossroads* by Ervin Laszlo
- *You Can Change the World* by Ervin Laszlo

FULLY ALIVE

Transformation requires
safety, science and a touch of the sacred.
Anything less, and what we get is incremental change.

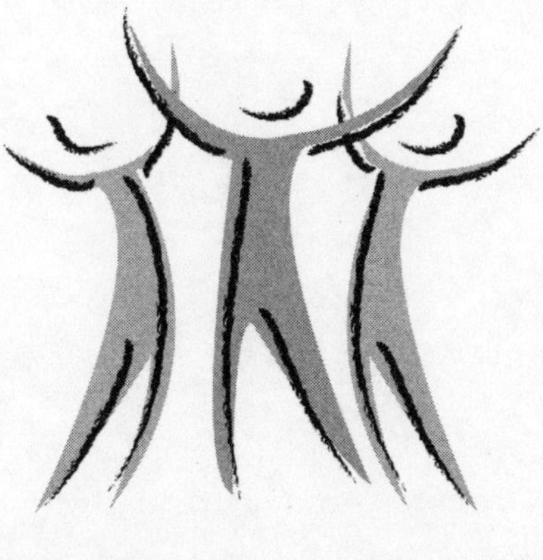

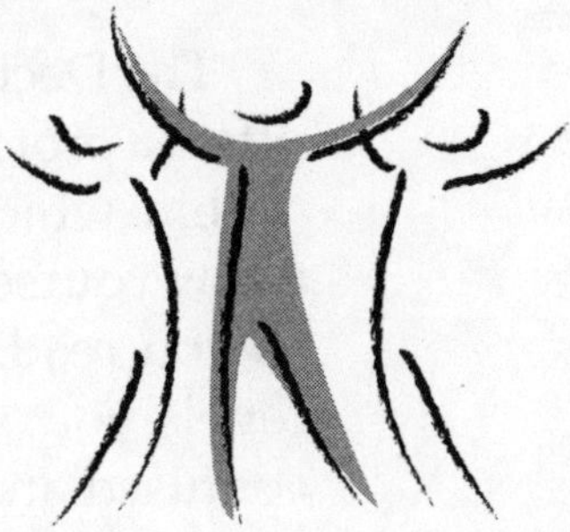

CHAPTER 8

A New Place To Stand

Every time I find myself writing about, speaking about or facilitating a conversation on 'ways to improve your life', I am reminded that *this has been* my life for more than 25 years. What an honor it is to be invited into the lives of so many who are seeking to find or to redefine themselves. In what becomes the Sacred Space of a shared enquiry, and as we discover just the right process to mid-wife new beginnings into the lives of so many, my own life is magically transformed. So here I sit, thinking to myself: what can I share with you that can make a difference in your life as you step into the coming pages? What will make it easier for you to manifest a meaningful life for yourself? After all, isn't that what we're looking for?

Transformation – although far too often over-promised and under-delivered! – is what I believe we are all looking for. Not incremental change; not small adjustments and little twists on the status quo, but those huge and irreversible changes to the way they move through the world. Our greatest invitation is to be able to free ourselves from our own limitations and experience the full potential of who we know, deep down inside, we truly are.

The Declaration of Evolution by Intention (Figure 10) offers a profoundly different and compelling new context within which to shape our lives. As you read below, allow yourself to pay attention to what occurs inside you as you read. Notice what you are drawn to and what repels you. Give yourself permission to be uncertain, confused and perhaps even agitated.

Notice the degree to which you are instinctively drawn to these provocative and compelling notions. Allow yourself to imagine living a life you design.

Declaration of Evolution by Intention™

In order to progress beyond historical notions of evolution through incremental change, to one of Evolution by Intention we must first:

- redefine who we are as human beings and how we experience our humanity; and
- rediscover and reclaim what has always been there, reawakening to our existing genius and potential to shape our world.

Who we must continue to become:

- Leaders of global transformation.
- An opportunity to engage life differently through:
  - A call to women to lead and co-create with men differently;
  - An invitation for men to relax into new ways of being;
- A 'wave' or 'movement' for creating living, organic collectives that thrive on the uniqueness of the individual and his/her impact when choosing to 'Engage!'
- A living model for manifestation of a future based on standing in the moment, looking into the future and creating by intention.

How we must choose:

We choose to make the choices that will move us toward our declared intention and to not make choices that will simply move us away from our fears.

Our declared beliefs/values/attitudes:

- History (the past) is irrelevant as a guide to creating the future.
- I live in a holographic universe
- I am a Quantum Biological Human
- Growth is a biological imperative
- I am critical to making a difference
- It's not too late
- I am up to the challenge
- There is an urgency to engage
- If not me, then who?
- This is fun, exciting and adventurous: I don't have to do serious things, seriously
- I am the godforce expressing in a physical universe
- My world is a safe and abundant place
- My confusion is a gateway/portal to my own evolution
- I am not alone
- My 'reality' is malleable based on my expectations
- What you think of me is none of my business
- Every response is an intelligent response: there are no exceptions!
- Your judgments of me are reflections of your internal landscapes
- When I engage, a difference occurs.
- My power is in the size and courage of my questions.

Figure 10: Declaration of Evolution by Intention™

This magnitude and depth of change need not be difficult. Nor does it have to take a long time! What I've discovered for myself is what I choose to share with you at this departure into the journey of your own personal evolution. But don't take my word for it. Try it on and see how it fits in your life.

- **Trust your body!** Your body never lies. Unlike what many of us have been taught to believe, not only is your body not the enemy, it is in fact the gateway to the transformation that we seek. Far more powerful than any process of the intellect, your body is the quantum biological processor that creates all the feelings/emotions that shape the experience of your life – and since it created them, it knows exactly what to do with them. All we need to do is surrender the intellect to the body and let the body lead. Our greatest challenge is getting out of our own way!

- **Breathe!** Science now tells us that your body is a quantum biological instrument of immense capability. It is not 'like' a bioprocessor – it "IS" a bioprocessor and breathing is what makes it possible for it to do its best work. Begin by paying attention to your breathing and notice when you hold your breath. In that moment, just stop…..close your eyes….and take three or four long, slow, deep breaths. If you extend the exhale so that it is twice as long as the inhale, you'll go a long way to creating a deep state of relaxation in the body. In that state, you cannot feel fear – and when we are unafraid, we are more willing and able to consider new information and new experiences.

- **Follow the Impulse!** The next time your body 'feels' something, instead of trying to shut down or move away from that sensation/impulse, breathe; relax your body; and choose to move into the sensation rather than away from it. Keeping your body open and relaxed, allow the sensation to begin to flow and to fill your body, all the time focusing your attention on keeping your body open and relax. You pay attention to your body and your body will pay attention to the energy/information that is moving. What you've been taught to call 'emotions' are really waves of energy/information trying to be metabolized (like your lunch) in the quantum biological processor that your body is, so that you can get on with your life! With the integration of each wave of information come insights and discoveries. Life changes – quickly, easily, effortlessly - and there is no going back.

- **Tell the truth of your experience!** Even if you never say it out loud to another soul, tell yourself the truth – inside you, where you live. Allow yourself to know the truth of your own experience. We lie to ourselves all the time and tell ourselves that something doesn't matter, when it does; that we're willing to do something when we're not; or that we want something when we don't. When we allow ourselves to claim the truth of our own experience, something powerful happens inside of us and in that moment, we discover more of our own potential. Yet consider, as much as you *need* never tell another soul, remember this: *Telling yourself the truth is an act of courage. Telling your truth out loud to another human being is an act of transformation.*

call out

- **Stay in the tough conversations!** The toughest conversation you'll ever have to stay in is the one with yourself. When you consider that there are only two things going on in the world - the conversations you have with yourself, and the conversations you have with another human being (i.e. chats, email, reports, etc); and when you consider that you can't change the one you have with another person unless and until you're both willing and able to change the one you have with yourself, staying in that tough conversation with YOU will determine the quality of your life! It will also determine your capacity for intimacy and connection to another human being because if you can't stay connected to you in a meaningful way, how can you ever connect to someone else in a meaningful way?

- **Be willing to stand alone!** That doesn't mean that you'll have to stand alone, you just need to know that if push comes to shove and you have to, you're both willing and able to do so. Far too often in life we go along just to get along, We compromise ourselves because we think that if we really let others see who we are, they'll move away from us. And yet, when we do that, we end up not liking ourselves much and have already moved away from ourselves. When we become both willing (a choice) and able (see the previous four points) to stand alone, we discover as we look around that there are many others who seek the same quality of life. These folks indeed, make great playmates!
- **Shape or be shaped by your world!** If you don't determine who you are, how you want to live and who you choose to become, you can be sure that someone else will do it for you. If you are not the game of your own choosing, you will likely become a game piece on someone else's board. It's not always easy to stay awake and define your life in a way that is meaningful to you – and it is always deeply gratifying.

So, take heart! Stop for a moment… take a nice, long, slow, deep breath… and step gently into your future, ready to discover the amazing Being that you are! You are not alone on this journey. As you decloak, allowing others to know of your curiosity and your search, you'll find yourself in good company.

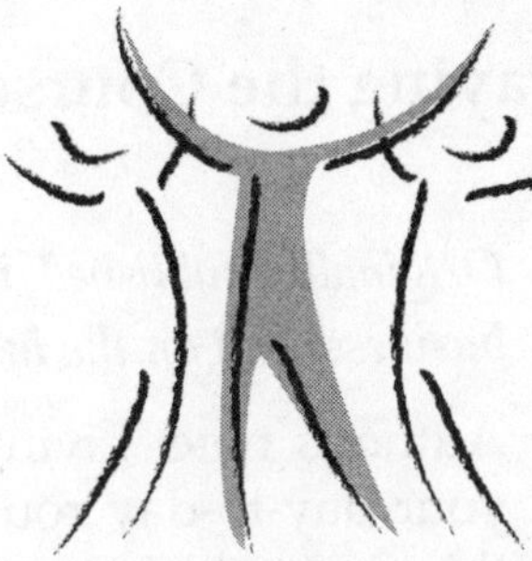

APPENDIX

Collection of Articles

This appendix contains a sampling of articles written by Louise LeBrun that have been published in other media. Covering a range of topics, they are an invitation to you to pay attention to how you think about the things you think about, noticing that when you change your thinking first, life becomes much easier to manage.

The articles that follow are:

- ***Staying the Course***
  Leadership / Personal and Professional Development
- ***Humour: The Missing Link in the Chain of Command***
  Leadership/Human Resource Management
- ***Levels of Thinking and the Chakras***
  Personal Growth / Spirituality
- ***Pathways to Personal Power***
  Leadership / Personal Expression
- ***NLP: Yesterday, Today and Tomorrow***
  Shifting Sands and New Paradigms
  Introduction to NLP

These articles and more are also available on the internet at www.WEL-Systems.com. They may be reproduced on condition of full acknowledgement of authorship and their location at the WEL-Systems Institute website and/or this book.

Staying the Course

Originally published in "In Pursuit" magazine, a publication for small business; and on the internet on CanadaOne (www.canadaone.com).

Author's note: Living a balanced life requires that you include, in your day-to-day routine, not only the things you must do but the things in which you find joy and delight. The following piece was written specifically for "Staying the Course" of a dream to create a successful business. Identify your dream and fill in the blanks, following the same principles to help you 'stay the course' of your intentions and take you to where you want to go. And remember - if you don't believe in yourself, why should anyone else?

It's been almost 10 years now, since I first started my own small business. All those romantic notions of independence, freedom and great wealth have been overtaken by long hours, hard work and the uncertainties brought by never knowing what tomorrow will bring. Sometimes, I long for the "good ole' days" and the paycheck, paid holidays and child-care leave that went with it.

And yet - truth be told - just like you, I wouldn't go back for all the money in the world! To build something from nothing; create and invent on a daily basis; and to contribute how, when and why I see fit are far greater rewards that I could ever have imagined. The key is to keep moving through and past those undeniable, inevitable moments of self-doubt and fear.

Home-based business operators often spend large chunks of time alone. Although telephone contact may be frequent, sometimes two or three days can go by without seeing another life form that has fewer than four legs. The end result is a sense of disconnection from the world. However, this sense of disconnection is minor compared to the sense of disconnection that I sometimes feel from myself: from my hopes and aspirations; from my plans; and from the very dream that started the whole thing, so long ago.

What I've learned over the years is that holding the dream is one thing - continuing to believe in my ability to breathe life into it is quite another. My greatest challenge has been to continue to believe in myself when others didn't; when the evidence in my bank statements, for all intents and purposes, screamed "Give it up!"; and when even my most ardent fans and supporters looked at me with great concern on their faces. Who would hold the dream?

If any of this rings true for you, perhaps the following thoughts will prove to be as meaningful for you as they have been for me. I share them with you with the hope that in your darkest moments, as they ebb and flow like the tides, you will remember to:

- Breathe! How easy it is to forget to breathe. Notice when you are holding your breath; and when your breathing has moved high up into the top of your chest. Whatever you are doing in that moment, STOP! Sit back in a chair; make a conscious decision to drop your shoulders, put your feet flat on the floor; let your arms hang loose by your sides, and take three, long, deep breaths. Focus all your attention on the sound of your own breathing moving in and out of your body. As you hear this sound, know that the Life Force is present, moving and vital; and that as you invite it to move freely through you, you will know exactly what to do.
- Pay attention to the impulses in your body. Notice where your attention is drawn; let your attention go to those places in your body where you are aware of sensations: the knot in your stomach; the tightness in your throat; the knit of your brow. Breathe directly into these places and allow yourself to notice whatever sounds or images come to mind. Use your breath to move into the information, expand that area of the body, and open and release that information into the larger system, meaning the entire body. Your whole body is the instrument that thinks.
- And finally, allow yourself to know the truth. Even if you never utter a word to another soul, or share this truth with anyone in any way, let yourself - deep inside you - know what is true for you. As you embrace and honor this truth, you will begin to notice that the images and the sounds move and change. As they do, become aware of your desire to contribute; to make a difference; to have

meaning in your life; to care. And as that vision that caused you to become who you are today begins to reform, allow all of those other images and sounds to melt into it. Keep your body open and relaxed - and breathe.

What it has taken me many years to come to understand is that the very thoughts I feared were the ones that held the greatest value. When I allowed myself to hold those thoughts, and let them move through my body, they became the markers on the road into the future. I leave you with the following thought, to guide you along your path.

"Everyone has talent. What is rare is the courage to follow the talent to the dark place where it leads".

Erica Jong

This article is available online at:
www.wel-systems.com/articles/staying.htm

Humor: The Missing Link in the Chain of Command

First published on the World Wide Web on the CanadaOne site (www.canadaone.com). This article has been recognized with an SBFocus.com Award (Atlanta, Georgia — www.smallbusinessarticles.com) as the best human resources article in the field of small business and entrepreneurship, published on the internet for April/99. Also published in the NATCON PAPERS (National Consultation on Career Development), an international publication; and most recently published in Optimum, the magazine for public service executives in Canada.

For many of us, work has become a place where things aren't very funny. Often, the first thing to go is the very thing that helps us go the distance: humor! What is it about humor that makes life easier to live? Why is it that something can be funny one day and leave you flat the next? What is the connection between humor and health, vitality and the ability to keep on truckin'? And most importantly, how good are you at noticing the things in your life - right now! - that are worthy of a good laugh!?

Work is a place where we have been taught to rely on our 'heads'; our intellects; our capacity to think things through and reason things out. Often, in order for us to do this successfully, we have to put aside what's going on inside our bodies; what we're feeling; what our instincts are telling us. We push down and push away the information that the body carries so that we can make reasonable, logical and rational choices, based on our analysis.

In order to do this effectively, we must abandon the process of the body. That means we have to move away from the tightening in the gut, the throbbing in the chest, the constriction in the throat, or the pounding in the ears. We have to learn to detach from the body and focus all of our attention on the process of the intellect, reminding ourselves that analysis is the pathway to effective living. At least, that's what we've been taught.

But things are changing rapidly today, with the advances of science. As we move away from a traditional allopathic perspective and venture into a quantum biological world-view, the lay of the land begins to move and sway, leaving us with a sensation not unlike an earthquake. Those very things which we have for so long considered to be solid, to be real, and to be the structures of our reality, begin to fade into movement and sway.

What does all this have to do with work and humor? Plenty! All this is about who we are as human beings; how we process information and make decisions; how our central nervous system works; and how, in the blink of an eye, our bodies move massive amounts of information that result in our insights, or intuition or sense of certainty about something. To understand this new science is to understand how human beings experience and express. And given that there is nothing going on at work but individual human beings interacting with each other, removing the film from the eyes through which we view this experience could mean the difference between coming alive or staying numb, at work.

And that includes humor. What is humor, anyway? Think about the last time that you found something to be funny. What is it about something that makes one person laugh uproariously, and leaves someone else flat, staring blankly and looking annoyed? What is it that determines whether or not we should laugh or cry? Not our intellects, for sure, since we've all had the experience of trying to explain a joke to someone, only to be met with that same vacant stare.

Where humor happens (or doesn't!) is in the body. When that laugh moves from your belly through your throat, and brings with it the sound that can bring relief around the board room table, what is actually going on inside you? Think of the last time you laughed 'til you cried. Remember how your body felt? Remember how your muscles tightened and caused your body posture to shift and your presence to take on a whole, new shape? There's nothing intellectual about a good laugh!

Our work environments have become places that are not very safe anymore, for the people who work in them. Particularly since we continue to create organizational systems that are built on the parent-child model, we often find ourselves in reporting relationships at work that have something very familiar about them. The boss reminds me of mom or dad; or the experience of the presence of any authority is reminiscent of another time and place. And our bodies respond.

Humor is distinctly absent from the chain of command. But that's not news, is it, since most of us grew up in environments where Mom and Dad, or our teachers and religious leaders, didn't use a lot of humor when setting the rules and regulations that would eventually define who we become. Given that those are the systems that shaped us, why would it be any different at work which, after all, is where we all go to demonstrate everything we learned in those old parent-child models of home, school and church? Without making a conscious effort to choose something else, our habituated response would be simply to repeat what we know.

If we want to create work environments that support and sustain life, we must begin by recognizing that where life lives is in the body. (If you don't believe that, trying taking your intellect to work without your body!) Humor is a word that we use as shorthand to describe the experience of another kind of movement in the body. But it's all about the body. If you want to get a good idea of whether or not your work environments support life, begin to pay attention to the kind of humor - or lack thereof - that permeates your workplace. Are things easy and light? Or is your humor dark, often dismissive of someone or something? Is the humor barbed and cynical? Pretty good chance that if people are expressing and experience this kind of humor, their bodies are feeling the tension that goes along with it: tight, bracing against, feeling the need to attack and/or protect. It's tough to increase creativity and innovation in environments that are closed and confining.

And aren't creativity and innovation what we say we want? Aren't creativity and innovation the pathways to increased productivity? After all, creativity means bringing something into existence that does not already exist. You won't find that in the rules and regulations - you already have those.

We know that creativity and innovation are not driven by the process of the intellect. They are not linear and structured; they move in bursts and waves, not unlike the way a laugh moves through the body: bursts and waves. In order for humor to be present in the workplace, there has to be a sense of safety and acceptance: that it's OK to say what's on my mind; to say things that fly in the face of the status quo; to question the dogma and to challenge the rules; and that it's not about authority, it's about creating and contributing and making a difference.

Given that we continue to structure organizations that rely on the parent-child model, its natural fall-out is a preoccupation with the notion of control. In our family systems, the parents were in charge and the kids weren't. At work, the boss (parent) is in charge and the employee (child) isn't. If the employee questions the views of the boss, or the direction that the boss is taking, that's like the children challenging the parents' right to control. Funny though, what we're learning today is that even in the family system, that model of expression and interaction is collapsing. Command and control don't cut it anymore. The children are growing up and are frequently far better educated and informed than the parents.

If we can recognize that this is happening at work, too, we can change the way we do business. If we can move away from the command and control model for our organizational 'leaders', we can begin to breathe a little easier in our workplaces. A conversation about the rules and the regulations and the dogma is just that - a conversation. It is not necessarily a tossing down of the gauntlet with corporate survival hanging in the balance.

If you want to create work environments that support and sustain life, start by making friends with what's going on inside of you. What makes you laugh? Or what stops you from laughing? Are your efforts at humor open and inclusive, or are they behind closed doors and dismissive of the people you work with? Pay attention to what goes on inside your own body; when your guts tighten and your lips form a tight, straight line. Pay attention to when you are holding your breath, and bracing against the sounds inside you that are pressing to get out. And pay particular attention to how frequently the things that annoy you at work, and/or the people that annoy you at work, and rob you of your capacity for ease, comfort, openness and humor, often have something very familiar about them. Search through what's inside you to find the match with what's going on outside of you, and notice how frequently old patterns and old habits have a way of just showing up.

Humor is the missing link in the chain of command. To put humor back into our workplaces would mean that we would have to put it back into our personal lives. To bring back to the workplace the capacity to laugh out loud and relax into those bursts and waves, would require that we relinquish our intense need for predictability and control, and make way for the uncertainty that precedes our greatest discoveries. As Ilya Prigogine once said: "The future is uncertain... but this uncertainty is at the very heart of human creativity".

When we were growing up, we didn't have much choice. If you're five years old, and you're in an environment that does not support life, you can't just get a job, an apartment and leave town. You are captive to your environment. But when you're 25, the rules have changed. And you can walk, and go where the breath moves more easily through the body. And isn't that exactly what we are dealing with today?

In today's environments, it's not just money that keeps people at work. More and more, companies are being forced to offer workplace conditions and contexts that support life overall: not just on the job, but in the area of personal wellness and quality of life. Employees are becoming much better educated and informed about what ties them down and what doesn't; and our old ways of doing business are falling away and being replaced by recognition that the contribution itself is what matters; and you can contribute and have fun at the same time! We are learning that we do not need to do serious things, seriously. That work can be play, and that play can be extremely productive.

The kids are growing up!

Steps to bringing humor back into the chain of command:

1. Lighten up! Today's effective executives/managers/supervisors are the ones who recognize that they are facilitators, not controllers. Managers manage environments; people manage themselves.
2. At your next staff meeting, ask people: What's it like for you to work here? What's it like when you wake up on Monday morning, and know that it's time to come back to work? And then listen, not only with your ears, but with your heart and soul and spirit. Breathe deeply into your body and choose to keep your body open and relaxed.
3. Sometimes, there's nothing else to do. Listening at those multiple levels is often what's missing to make life better at work. In our experience in working in organizational systems, what we have often found is that people feel unseen and unheard; feel invisible and dismissed. For most of us, what we really want is to feel that we are a part of something; that it matters that we show up at work; and that someone notices when we don't.
4. Find the things at work that drive you crazy and notice where else they happen in your life. The next time those buttons get pushed, instead of bracing against them and pushing them back, breathe right into them and let them move: like bursts and waves in the body. We now know from science that what we call an emotion or a feeling is actually movement of information and energy through the body; a transfer of information and intelligence through biochemical and electrochemical impulses. That movement is a sign of life.
5. Laughter is a sign of life. What kind of signals are you putting out to the people around you?

This article is available online at:
www.wel-systems.com/articles/humour.htm

Levels of Thinking and the Chakras

This article was originally published in the Journal of the American Board of Neuro-Linguistic Programming, Fall '97, PP. 3 - 5. The original content has continued to be developed to form the basis for The CODE Model™. .

Additional information related to this article is available on the audio tapes 'Pathways to Personal Power' (see product/program pages at the end of the book).

The following article presumes a working knowledge of both Logical Levels and the chakras. For those of you who would appreciate information in greater detail, there is much literature available on both subjects. My personal favorites are Robert Dilts for Logical Levels, and Anodea Judith and Caroline Myss for the Chakras.

Also, in the interests of both time and space (illusions though they may be!), it will become obvious that the extensive thought processes that gave rise to these insights have been abbreviated. My intention is not to give you answers, but to share the questions.

Your brain, as well as any other biological or social system, is designed to process information in varying chunks, or levels. These levels represent information processing from the very general to the very specific - or vice versa. Your brain has a predictable way of processing this information that relates to both the experience of thinking and that of being.

In the NLP community, the original thinking about these "logical levels" was that there were five levels of processing, each encompassed in the level above it. They are best described in the words of Robert Dilts:

"From the psychological point of view there seem to be five levels that you work with most often. (1) The basic level is your environment, your external constraints. (2) You operate on that environment through your behavior. (3) Your behavior is guided by your mental maps and your strategies, which define your capabilities. (4) These capabilities are organized by belief systems and (5) beliefs are organized by identity."

Since this work was done in 1990, these levels have evolved to include a sixth, spirituality. I invite you to consider the possibility that there is a seventh logical level so subtle that it has gone undetected, as it is the larger context within which several of the other levels unfold.

We know that we presume there to be seven major chakras. Over the past seven years of working in programs and individually with clients, particularly when I was working with the chakras, I'd notice that there were seven chakras and only six Logical Levels. How could this be? I was struck by the correspondence between the chakras and the Logical Levels, and felt certain that a pattern must be completing itself. As I played with it over the years, things began to fall into place.

The following very abbreviated and simple journey through the chakras and Logical Levels may encourage you to consider the correspondences for yourself.

The Root chakra is about being grounded. Naturally, it corresponds to the earth element. We believe that the very light, very fast energies move down from the Crown chakra through to the Root chakra, manifesting thought in physical space and time. It makes perfect sense that there is a connection between the earth element, the Root chakra and the experience of our personal, physical surroundings in their myriad manifestations. (Logical Level - Environment: Where and When.).

The second chakra is the seat of emotion in the body, often referred to as the watery area. Feelings are held in this part of the body. The element here is water, magnetic and with the power to draw to us experiences which allow us to notice the emotions that are held captive in there. Our behaviors are driven by our emotional states. Our sense of resourcefulness or resourcelessness leads to specific behaviors. (Logical Level - Behaviors: What)

The third chakra, the Power chakra, is the center of the ability to take action. It is from this area that I experience the energy that powers my capacity to act. The fuel (and the element) is fire, combustible and resulting in movement, either slow (embers) or rapid (explosions). The conduit for the expression of this energy - what forms the channel through which this energy can flow - is my capability, meaning my ability to determine the appropriate course of action into which to direct the powerful force of movement. (Logical Level - Capability: How)

And here's where things get interesting. The fourth or Heart chakra is considered to be the center of identity - but at what level? My belief is that the Heart chakra is the center of who I think I am; that collection of beliefs, values and attitudes that are the by-product of habituated responses and early cultural conditioning. But is it really who I am, or just who I think I am? Or worse, who I have been taught to believe that I am? The element associated with this chakra is the air element. Air represents movement and change. If the chakra is open and air is moving freely, then my beliefs are subject to movement and change, thus allowing for and ensuring growth and expansion. If the chakra is closed, or if my heart is closed, my beliefs, values and attitudes are like concrete - and have become immovable. We even talk about how the heart hardens, or turns to stone.

The fifth chakra is the Throat chakra, the seat of self-expression, the gateway for revealing who I am to the world. It is the way that I make myself heard in the universe. The element associated with this chakra is sound (sound waves). The sounds that we make, through speech or through the symbol of speech - the written word - are the physical impressions of our presence in the world.

The sixth chakra is the Third Eye, the center of ethereal sight. Through and with it, we can see beyond what is to what can be. The element associated with this chakra is light (light waves).

The seventh chakra is the Crown chakra, the center of spirituality, where we connect to something greater than our experience in the body. It is the point of entry of "source" energy into the various levels of the body. It is the point of contact between what I experience as "me" and the larger context of I AM. The element associated with this chakra is thought.

My belief is that the Logical Level of Beliefs, Values and Attitudes corresponds to the fourth or Heart chakra; that the level of Identity corresponds to the sixth chakra or the Third Eye; and that at the fifth chakra or Throat chakra lies the as-yet unnamed Logical Level of Choice (Which).

Whether we are conscious of it or not, we are always choosing. When we are silent, our absence of speech is a choice. Over the last years, I have been struck by two things in my programs: how common it is that people do not recognize they are choosing and that there are never any exceptions; and also that all behaviors have consequences, whether we notice them or not. So change does mean consequences, but there are also consequences associated with no change. This underlying process was completely transparent to those who were doing the choosing. Yet, at each of the Logical Levels, we are choosing.

I believe that at the Heart chakra level we carry the past of who we have been conditioned and taught to believe we are. We carry the conditioned responses that manifest through those beliefs, values and attitudes. And I believe that at the Third Eye, we carry the potential to "see" who we are capable of becoming; to recognize grace and perfection as our birthright; and to hold that as a model or standard for expression. At the level of the Third Eye, we can know our own magnificence.

The throat is the gateway to sound; it is the junction of the internal and the external; it is the point at which information from the Heart chakra collides with information from the Third Eye and its messages of possibility and magnificence. It is there where I must choose which will direct my life. It is there where this struggle is resolved and the resolution is put forward, into physical space and time, for all to hear and know; it is the point at which I either choose to decloak and move toward who I AM, or to stay cloaked, to await the next opportunity for expression - with these opportunities never-ending.

The first through the fourth chakras carry history; the sixth and the seventh carry possibility. The fifth chakra, at the throat, is the link between these points in time as well as the platform on which we stand in the "now". This platform is my connection to what I perceive as the outside world. As I stand on this platform in the present, do I speak from history or do I speak from possibility? As I choose mindfully, information from the higher chakras moves into the lower ones, disengaging me from multiple dualities and allowing for the integration, in the full body, of new insights.

The throat is the point at which we choose either to continue to repeat our experience or choose to make different sounds and create a new expression of ourselves. Do I continue to express myself from the Heart chakra, which carries history and training, or do I express my Self from the Third Eye, which holds and defines what I am divinely capable of? Do I express in a way that I always have-do I say yes when I want to say no because it is the nicer thing to do-or do I stand tall (notice the sixth chakra is physically higher in the body than the fourth) and express something that is much more a reflection of who I know my self to be - and to be capable of becoming.

If there is conflict between the fourth and the sixth chakras, there will likely be struggle in the throat. If the rules (in the fourth) always bump up against what I believe is possible (in the sixth) I get tension in the throat: which do I speak myself to be? When the path clears from the fourth through to the sixth, expression flows easily, smoothly - and is free to change as air moves through the fourth chakra, bringing new insights and awareness to beliefs, values and attitudes (for example, I have the right to change my mind.).

The throat is also located at the narrowest, and by extension, most fragile point in the physical body. Here, the spinal column and major arteries are at their least protected. In our decision to choose mindfully, we are at our most vulnerable and our most fragile. We risk taking what has been secret and making it public for all to hear, see and judge. We have laid ourselves bare.

This level of thinking has to be identified and articulated. It's huge in its implications, given that we are choosing at every level. The question then becomes: are we choosing mindfully, or are we mindlessly dancing to habituated responses? Positioning it at the level of the fifth chakra - a very high level - draws our attention to our vehicle for self-expression (sound and speech), as well as to the profound implications of choice, which are about identity, self, who I AM in the world.

Until we mindfully, consciously choose to be greater than our experience, our experience will be what defines who we are. And since our experience is limited, we too, will fall short of what holds power and possibility for us. To make choice a conscious, mindful volition at all Logical Levels is to bring out of the darkness the very act of power which, by default, is causing us to hold and maintain the status quo. Anything we can name, we can make real and visible in the universe. Once visible, its power can be tapped and expressed in a way that moves us even further into the Light.

Logical level	Chakra	ELEMENT
Spirituality *who else?*	Crown	Thought/Light
Identity *who?*	Third eye	Vision/Sight
Choice *which?*	Throat	Speech/Sound
Beliefs/Values/Attitudes *why?*	Heart	Air
Capability *how?*	Power	Fire
Behavior *what?*	Second Chakra	Water
Environment *where? when?*	Root	Earth

Please note that the word "element" is used loosely for purposes of drawing relationships among these three thought systems.

This article is available online at:
www.wel-systems.com/articles/chakra.htm

Pathways To Personal Power

Previously published in the NATCON PAPERS, a collection of summaries from conference presentations at the NATCON conference (1999), sponsored by the University of Toronto.

Pathways implies more than one way to get where you're going - and in the midst of career transition, you want that kind of choice. *Personal* means they're all inside you - and who better to depend on? And *Power* is about the result these internal pathways create: do they enhance your capacity to fully express yourself? Before you move on to unfold the next layer in your career evolution, take a moment to consider that your most powerful messages - like your greatest triumphs and darkest moments - all come from inside yourself. How well is your decoder working?

The notion of 'power' or, more specifically, personal power is one that captures the imagination. The dictionary defines power as the capacity to act. For what purpose? In what context? What exactly does it mean, in terms of quality of life? How do I become a person of great personal power? How would I be different from who I am now? Would I change the way I live my life? And if power is a force, where does that force come from? How would I direct that force and what kind of life would I create for myself and for the people around me?

Have you ever noticed that one of the more interesting things about power is that all of us think everybody has some - except ourselves! If you're the boss, you think the employees have it; and if you're the employees, you think the boss has it. If you're the parents, you know the kids must have it because you sure don't; and if you're the kids, you feel the need to fight for it since it certainly rests in the hands of the older generation. Why is it that power remains so elusive for so many? Why do we tend to think of power as something that exists outside of us, that we can earn or simply take, maybe even buy, and then wield like a weapon? How is it that we think of power as something finite, with only so much available and if someone else has some, we may not get enough;

that power is designed to be used to make things happen, to do things to something; and that, if you aren't very careful, someone will try to do something to you or make you do something you don't want to do? Or, perhaps, even take your power away? It is as if there were a shortage and we must zealously guard whatever we have for fear of its being taken or simply evaporating if we are not relentless in our vigilance.

Stripped of our sense of personal power - that is, our ability to create for ourselves a life that we want and believe to be worth living - we are left trembling in fear and uncertainty or filled with resentment and rage. We experience a deep sense of loss of dignity and a violation of our personal integrity (i.e. wholeness). If we react so profoundly to such an awareness, is it possible that personal power is a naturally occurring state and one which we hold, at some very deep level, to be our birthright?

The things that occur at very deep levels of the body, and/or deeper levels of mind, must move beyond linguistically structured thought, which is how we have been taught to think. Our cultural conditioning has kneaded and molded us to focus our attention on the words in our heads at the cost of the sensations in our bodies. For generations, and in a variety of ways, we have been conditioned to ignore our instinct and our intuition, and to abdicate to the rules and regulations of home, church and school. By the time we get to work, where we will spend more time than anywhere else in our adult lives, we are well trained. It's a miracle that we can feel anything at all!

By the time we get to work, we have been rewarded for close to two decades for *not* thinking for ourselves, but for toeing the party line; being a team player; not rocking the boat; and supporting the status quo. That powerful energy that ran through our bodies seems to have cut back to a trickle. And often, we find ourselves feeling flat and lifeless; bored and wondering, 'Is this all there is?; or agitated and impatient, not knowing why. Perhaps it's time we went deeper into our own awareness and went beyond what we have been taught to call 'reality' or 'truth'.

In Pathways to Personal Power, we take a journey into places where many people rarely allow themselves to go. We go deep into the self.... inside... where our feelings reside; our greatest hopes and our darkest fears. And we begin to notice that before life happens 'out there', it happens inside first. We begin to ask ourselves questions, such as: If I am so quick to take responsibility (i.e. hold myself able to respond) for the things in my life that are working, why am I am so quick to hold someone else responsible when it's not working? Why it is so easy for me to reach out and grasp the things that work yet so quick to drop the things that don't work, as if bitten by a snake? What if I am responsible (i.e. hold myself able to respond) for it all - the good and the bad; the stuff that works and the stuff that makes me want to crawl back into bed and stay there!

We begin the workshop by taking a journey into the evolution of the human being: how did we get to be who and how we are? We explore how - no matter your gender, your time and/or place of birth, your cultural conditioning, your religious training - there are certain structures and experiences common to all human beings.

The first of these is that we arrive, with the basic design being one of a number of organs, structures and systems in a 'bag' called the body; including a brain and a nervous system. We concede that we have learned more about the brain and the nervous system in the last ten years than we had known in the previous 100. This is not rocket science. You need read only the more popularized journals, like Discover or MacLean's or Time magazine, to find articles that marvel at the power of the human nervous system; at how with every new thought we think, the topography of the brain shifts, never again to think the same thoughts the same way. We know today that the brain and the central nervous system are living, breathing, shifting, changing and growing expressions of who we are; that as the tissue shifts and changes, so does our ability to process information. The human nervous system is recognized as the most magnificent bio-computer in the known universe, capable not only of astounding acts of repetition but also of massive waves of creativity and innovation. We all have a brain and a nervous system and as we come to better understand it and make friends with it, our capacity to fully express and create causes the world to be permanently altered.

In addition to having a body, a brain and a central nervous system, there are other things that we have in common, around the globe. For example, none of us is hatched. We all go through a process where we are conceived and grow in utero for, give or take, nine months. We all experience a birth process which is still either vaginal delivery or Caesarean section. We all have initial experiences with Mom and Dad, or our first contact with power and authority; we have extended family, including siblings, aunts, uncles and cousins, etc.; we have baby-sitters, in some way, shape or form; and we have community activities that begin at a very early age, like T-Ball, Cubs, Brownies or Sunday school. Today, we have daycare where children spend more time with relative strangers than they will ever spend with their own families. And then, of course, we have what I fondly refer to as boot camp for Life, or school; and let's not forget Church, or some form of religious structuring And finally, the one place you will spend more time than anywhere else in your life - work. Whether work takes place in the rice fields or on the 45th floor of a downtown high-rise, the effect is the same.

Deep inside us, each of us carries information unique to our structuring of the world in which we live. These experiences, from conception to death, are wired directly into the nervous system and literally shape who we become. Traditional psychologists believe that our core beliefs - meaning our beliefs about ourselves (good person, bad person); our beliefs about the world (safe, unsafe) and our beliefs about our ability to manage in our world (competent, incompetent) are in place by the time we are five years old. Having had two children and having worked with adults now for close to twenty years, I believe they are in place much earlier. Few of us ever revisit those core beliefs as structured and defined through the experiences of a five year old. Just ask yourself: when was the last time you thought about what you believe, about what really matters to you - not what someone else wants you to believe, or thinks you should believe, but what really matters to you? If it's been a while, you also have to ask yourself who's driving the bus.

Is it any surprise that we become adults and when certain circumstances present themselves, we feel like children? Have you ever wondered why it is that you are an intelligent, articulate, capable and responsible adult until you cross the threshold of your parents' house and then, all of a sudden, you're eight? What is stored inside us that leaves us believing in our own powerlessness and helplessness?

Although we have been trained to operate from what is referred to as linguistically structured thought - meaning that how we think the process of thinking occurs is in words and phrases - there is much more occurring inside the body. For hundreds of years, ancient wisdom has proffered the notion of energy centers in the body, or chakras, that are like generators that keep the body energy, or life force, moving freely. Many trained in the traditional allopathic world view have, until recently, dismissed this notion as ludicrous, as there was no evidence that could be measured with the naked eye or with existing instrumentation.

However, with the discoveries of scientists such as Candace Pert (*Molecules of Emotion*) or Valerie Hunt (*Infinite Mind: The Vibrations of Human Consciousness*), we are becoming more aware of the power of the human body and the implication of the presence of an electromagnetic field that surrounds it. There is a correlation between the movement of energy through this electromagnetic field, the process of thought as we have come to know it, the movement of energy and information through bio-chemical and electrochemical impulses through the body, and our sense of personal power. Given that few of us were taught any of this in Grade 10 biology/science classes; or even beyond at the University level, how well do we know how to decode the messages of the body and their relationship to our thoughts?

The next step in the program is to introduce a tool that we use not only for defining the relationship between linguistically structured thought and movement of energy, but also for decoding the messages of the energy system in the body and identifying their expression through linguistically structured thought. We explore how our cultural conditioning has taught us to ignore the messages from the body and defer to the rules, whatever they may be, at work, at home and in relationships. We have been taught to value linguistically structured thought, which often translates to logic and reason, above all else in our lives. But have you ever noticed that before you ever think a linguistically structured thought there is always a movement of energy through the body? We sometimes call that movement 'a hunch' or 'a gut feel'. And yet, as our thoughts become more habituated, we notice the energy less and less, as it has become a habit of thought and moves through deeply rooted existing pathways, with very little resistance from tissue in the body. Science tells us that the average human being thinks about 65,000 thoughts a day. That's the good news. The bad news is that more than 90% of them are exactly the same as the ones we thought yesterday!

As you allow yourself to think new thoughts, meaning to move away from the traditional, culturally conditioned, biased thinking, the topography of the brain is actually transformed by the action of this process and its related movement of energy. When this happens, a sensation runs through the body. You have just had an original thought or a new insight, or an interpretation that is entering your awareness for the first time. It is not unusual at such times to find yourself unable to put words to what you have just experienced. When this happens, you become able to perceive your experience through new eyes, to process the data of your life through new thought models. It is now impossible for you to come to the same old conclusions.

Personal power is the deep sense of calm and alignment that comes from knowing that you create your own reality. What matters is not what happens; what matters is what you do about it. Personal power is trusting, at a very deep level of mind, that no matter what is occurring in your experience, you created it. If you created it, you can change it and create something else instead. With this level of trust also comes a willingness to think new thoughts, take risks, say no to the things that hold no value for you and move forward. What also comes with this level of trust is a willingness and an ability to allow yourself to know the truth - not truth as an absolute but truth as it exists for you, from deep inside you where you live.

Your body is sending you messages all the time. You will interpret these messages through culturally conditioned thinking, which may result in your interpreting them as pain or the flu or a sinus headache. Were you to become more familiar with the energy centers in the body, you would come to realize, for example, that your headache is about the energy center called the Third Eye, which is the center of ethereal sight, the platform on which we stand to move into the future, or the center of the possible self. If you are experiencing pain, which is caused by a blockage of movement of energy, you may want to consider what is going on in your life with regard to your future. Are you allowing yourself to know the truth of where you want to go and what you want to do? Of who you want to become? Are you experiencing confusion about your next step in life and feeling uncertain about taking action? Are you trying to push away an insight that you know is there and, should you allow yourself to acknowledge it, you will no longer be able to live as you do? (For more detail, refer to Anodea Judith, "Wheels of Life".)

Each of these energy centers relates to a specific level of thinking, meaning that movement in each of the energy centers carries clues and cues about its corresponding level of linguistically structured thought. When you work with both of these together (integrating the process of the left brain and the right; or the processes of the conscious mind and the unconscious mind), you become aware of things that are sometimes hidden from view. Learning how to decode these messages could be the key to changing your life. There is no greater sense of power than to know that you are in control of your own destiny.

Take the big plunge and read Candace Pert, or Valerie Hunt or Anodea Judith. So what if they weren't recommended reading in high school or university! You may be surprised to know that science has made leaps and bounds since you and I were in our twenties! We are not who we have been taught to believe we are. We are multidimensional, multi-faceted expressions of pure potential. But sometimes, when we look in the mirror, we'd never know it

This article is available online at:
www.wel-systems.com/articles/power.htm

NLP: Yesterday, Today and Tomorrow
Shifting Sands and New Paradigms

Part I
NLP – Yesterday

Introduction

NLP has come a long way. Over the last 30 years, who could estimate how many have been touched – intentionally or otherwise – by this incredible discovery of the structure of human behavior. And yet, despite these amazing contributions, there are nonetheless those for whom NLP has not been enough. There are many who have studied and applied the knowledge of NLP, at all levels of certification, only to discover that they continue to be taken hostage by something greater; and that the tools and techniques of NLP have not offered the portals and passages that allow them to engage the world differently and – even more – to shape it.

As the years have rolled by and one century has passed into the next, little attention has been paid to what we have taken for granted for close to four decades. The vast majority of advances in NLP have been refinements within the body of knowledge itself and not discoveries in its connections and relationships to other advances in the field of human potential. As a metaphor, this is akin to continuing to explore and perfect motor vehicle transport as a mechanical device without considering the advances in electronics. In any other field of endeavor, this would be considered at best, folly and at worst, a recipe for missed opportunities.

Now is as good a time as any to stop and consider not just the content of what we know but the context within which we have learned it, expressed it and passed it on to others. The 21st Century not only invites but demands that we reconsider both the practice and the potential that NLP offers. Since all meaning is context dependent, this shift in perspective is essential to continuing growth and evolution in the application of NLP; and for sustaining

NLP as a viable and practical resource in the transformation of our species. It has been said that "Before we can change our lives, we must first change the way that we perceive our lives."[1]

This shift in perspective will be framed by two notions from NLP: Logical Levels of Thinking and Representational Systems….. with one very big difference. Instead of six rep systems and six logical levels, we will work with seven.

Logical Levels of Thinking, or neurological levels, has formed part of this body of knowledge for some time and has proven to be a very useful tool. The tool is always, in some way, a creation of the artist in recognition of a requirement for the expression of that artistry. Logical Levels of Thinking is no different.

The first six Levels of Thinking, as developed by Bateson and Dilts, have been extremely effective in ordering information. However, human beings are organic. Our ability to choose differentiates us from each other as well as from other 'life' forms. Unlike your car which cannot choose to become a motor cycle, human beings can choose, at any time, to be and do other than what is currently available. As far back as 1997, we added and began working with the seventh Logical Level of Choice (between Beliefs/Values/Attitudes and Identity), taking that which has always been present and yet transparent to the process and bringing it to conscious awareness. By bringing the act of choosing 'out of the closet' so-to-speak, we acknowledge the ability of human beings to shape their experience. We create a platform for choosing that also makes it impossible to deny that we are indeed, doing so; and acknowledges the power of its presence … and the natural by-product of its expression, whether conscious or otherwise. We are always choosing, whether we do so with focused intention (design) or from habit (default or fall-back position).[2]

---

1 Trick of the Light

2 Refer to "The Seventh Logical Level of Thinking: choosing with purpose, power and intention" by Louise LeBrun; NLP World, November 2001, Volume 8, No.3

With this discovery came the willingness to play with other things which appeared fixed and were indeed, mutable. From six representational systems (visual, auditory, kinesthetic, olfactory, gustatory, auditory digital) came a seventh: PsI, or PsychicIntuitive. In creating this seventh, we acknowledge that a continuum exists, with auditory digital (or the absence of sensory cues) at one end and PsychicIntuitive (the presence of all sensory cues) at the other end. Like black and white represent this phenomenon, so representational systems can easily be enhanced to reflect this in the world of sensory input. [3]

Looking back

"All meaning is context dependent". We must have said those words at least a thousand times over. Yet, how often have we actually stopped… and considered the profound implications of their meaning in how we live – and teach – NLP?

The Communication Model of NLP identifies a variety of filters through which we process information and the power that these filters carry to shape what we do and don't allow ourselves to consider. The primary filter is that of Space/Time/Matter/Energy… the filter through which we consider what we hold as true and 'real' about the very shape and structure of our physical world and our presence in it. Science – the god of the culture – tells us what is 'true' about space/time/matter/energy and from that 'truth', we proceed to interact in our world. We have learned not to argue with science!

Being the voracious creatures that we are for MORE, our sense of curiosity and adventure has taken us down unknown paths and into brave, new worlds. We have discovered more in the last 20 years than we had in the 100 before that. Our ability to learn and then build on that learning has allowed us to move through the world in a way that invites the miracles of technology that we experience today. The cars we drive to work and play will, in the

3 Refer to "WEL-Systems® : The New Paradigm for NLP: A Non-therapy context for change" by Louise LeBrun; Rapport, Winter 2001

not-so-distant future, be driving us! The planes we fly now have the ability to move in and out of the earth's atmosphere… and beyond. Our technological advances allow for magic and miracles in medicine, communication, entertainment, transportation… the list goes on and on.

The things we once held to be true – and unquestionably so – have time and again been proven not so much to be untrue but to be constrained by our ability to perceive them in their wholeness. Take, for example, Kirlian photography. Now exceeding 50 years since its discovery, there was a time when this ability to detect electromagnetic fields around the body through image, did not exist. Does that mean that the field was not there? Absolutely not. What did not yet exist was our ability to detect it. What we needed was a new framework within which to detect this phenomenon and then consider our discovery.

Think of all those poor souls who burned at the stake because their internal 'camera' allowed them to detect these fields… these auras of light and color … around living things. Think of other times and other places when we have dismissed as untrue or non-existent that which was only out of the range of detection. It was there. We just could not 'represent' it in ways that matched the current context or paradigm of thought.

NLP began to unfold in just such a context. The science of the time was grounded in a Newtonian perspective… or context. Grinder and Bandler, through a process of external calibration (observation) and internal calibration (questions), were able to nudge into awareness that which had always been there and yet had gone undetected. Using the combination of observation and enquiry, they created a platform for 'modeling' (or replicating) that which was already present and not yet generalized.

This process was unique and different. For the first time, we were able to consider human behavior beyond the level of content (I said, you said, he/she did, etc.) and consider human interactions in a different light. The claim was made that NLP did not engage human behavior at the level of content but at the level of structure.

We held the ability to notice and make distinctions at this level to be one which freed us from content and allowed us to affect change directly by interplay with the structure itself.

The one thing we did not ask was: what is the context for this notion of structure? All meaning is context dependent.

The Science of the early '70's – which determined who we believed human beings to be and more importantly, who we believed them to be capable of becoming – was deeply rooted in Newtonian principles. This was the science of predictability in physical realms; the science of norms and standards and range of operation based on physical realities. This science has spawned the 'therapy' model of the world, which has permeated and shaped all that we have known and touched. To ask someone to consider that the therapy model, with its norms and standards and limited range, was not 'truth' but a limited context based on the limitations of our knowledge, would be like asking the fish "How's the water?" The context for considering the question was the subject itself, with no consideration for 'not water' available at that time. The ability for a larger context did not exist.

Things have changed

Science has moved in leaps and bounds to invite us to consider magic and miracles as every day occurrences. The science of even 10 years ago, let alone 30 years ago, invited consideration of new things and yet had not begun to shine bright lights on the dark little spaces and places of who we thought ourselves to be. We've come a long way, Baby….and we're moving fast into an amazing future!

To reiterate, the vast majority of advances in NLP have been refinements within the body of knowledge itself (Environment/Behavior/Capability) and not discoveries in its connections and relationships to other advances in the field of human potential (Spirituality). Given that within the framework of Logical Levels, every level is contained in the levels above it; and those changes at higher levels of thinking flow through and alters lower levels, imagine what becomes possible if we reconsider NLP within that higher level of thinking.

How can we take the principles of the quantum sciences and apply them not just to our technologies and gadgets and 'things', but to our own evolution as organic, living systems? How do we take what we now know about the science of who we are as human beings; the science of energy and potential, and make our potential come alive within the limitlessness that it offers? How do we take what we now know from science – the knowledge that we are quantum biological processors, capable of moving information/ energy at incredible rates and in huge amounts – and apply this to how we live our lives, every single day, and to how we affect the lives of those we touch?

How do we take NLP – originally set in a Newtonian context, a 'therapy' model context – and bring it to life in the new paradigm of expression that we have already become… and have yet to notice? Is it not time to consider that NLP may better serve us all if it were to keep pace with science? Could it be that the potential of NLP will expand exponentially when considered in a new context? Given that all meaning is context dependent, what meaning will NLP take on when considered within an autopoietic framework and a model of the world that says that human beings are not mechanistic devices but quantum biological instruments of expression?

The thing that is most enticing is not 'what can we become'. The thing that is most incredible to consider is: what have we **already** become … and have yet to notice?

If all meaning is context dependent, what is the context that we have held for NLP to this time? NLP can only expand within the limitations of our ability to consider it. As we expand the context within which we position NLP, its potential will expand accordingly.

In its existing context or paradigm, NLP came into being within the science of the day and our beliefs about the nature of being human. NLP as a body of knowledge was 'built' and has been sustained within the context of human beings and their behavior (.e. a therapy model). What if we were to consider NLP within the context of human beings as quantum biological devices – organic computers – (i.e. an autopoietic model)? What potential now sits, unexplored, and invites our attention?

Part II
NLP – Today

Space, Movement and Flow

Consider, for a moment, the power of emptiness. The notion of Space, boundless and limitless in its potential to allow for things to unfold; and its ability to make room not only for what's already there to expand but for what else may come. Consider, for a moment, that when Space is available, it becomes the invitation for 'things' to move into it… to flow through it… to be engaged. As we create Space – in our physical world as in our emotional/spiritual/psychological worlds – new things come into our lives. As we create Space in the way we think, our minds and our lives open to new ideas and their accompanying potential. Without Space, there is no movement.

In the realm of Space/Matter/Time/Energy, our notions of 'reality' have been challenged by the New Science and shaken to their very foundations. What we once held as 'real' and 'true' now exist as possibilities only and some things that we had held as absolutes have disappeared entirely. With the shifting of these sands come new ways of being in the world and new ways of 'seeing' what we once saw through the eyes of limitation and ignorance.

Owners Manual for the Body – Awakening to the Self

In a quantum biological age, we are discovering that human beings are far more than we had ever considered possible. The body, which we once believed to be who we are, we now know to be a quantum biological processor (QBP). Organic, brilliant, immeasurable in its potential, with the ability to detect and calibrate for 'energy' at levels that defy our understanding or appreciation… but processors, nonetheless. This is not my personal opinion. – its science.

We already know that the human body is far more than we had ever dreamed it to be. Today's science demonstrates that our bodies are bio-processors. They are not analogous to a bio-processor, or metaphorically bio-processors, but ARE bio-processors. With a sensing and processing capability that defies our ability to comprehend, our bodies move through the world on our behalf, tracking at 4 billion bits of information per second, and yet only drawing our attention to the things that we have determined to be meaningful.

We know that our bodies, these QBP's, are the instrument through which we move in space/time, in a physical world. Without them, we may be detectable to a limited few but would miss the opportunity to be the life of the party! Without them, we would never know the taste of chocolate; or the smell of the ocean; or the feel of a warm, evening breeze brush across our skin. Our bodies allow us to be perpetually sensing in a boundless and limitless world of sensory input – both external and internal. They allow us to make distinctions in experience that we would miss were we not able to calibrate with such precision and expand our expression as a result of it.

NLP is a body of knowledge that was originally developed through a process of observation and enquiry. What made it so unique in its time was that it did not seek to understand any particular story (content) but sought to document the structure of how the story was being expressed through the mechanism of the body. This included functions that could be calibrated externally (i.e. eye patterns and language) as well as those that could be tracked internally (i.e. strategy). These distinctions allowed us to begin to see the correlation of the external and the internal.

NLP helps us to understand how the mechanism of the body functions. In the truest sense of the word, the body of knowledge of NLP operates at the Environment Level of Logical Levels, providing an 'owner's manual' for the way the mechanism of the body functions. We can then move away from the content of behavior and use the functions of the mechanism to recognize and acknowledge how the behavior is expressed through the mechanism.

For example, eye patterns are an indicator to us of how 'the mouse' is seeking to locate information in various files. We can generalize and say that if the 'mouse' is moving up and to the left, it is seeking information considered 'remembered' and stored in images. If the 'mouse' is seeking information that we are creating and doing so in sound, the eyes will move to the right, mid level. Predictable in terms of both function and intent.

NLP will also help us to understand that the body (bio-processor) has an ability to either reduce (Auditory digital) or accelerate (Psychic Intuitive) the speed at which information moves through the mechanism (processing speed). Again, by way of example, if we slow the processing speed, we can take a 'memory' (keeping in mind that 'memory' is a nominalization) and can calibrate for details on how that particular memory is stored. We can also increase the processing speed (in therapy model terms, an insight/gestalt) so that the information moves so quickly we are unable to detect and calibrate for content. In the language that we've created, we consider the slow processing speed to be at the Ad (Auditory digital) end along a continuum, and the fastest processing speed on that continuum to be at what we've called the Psychic Intuitive (or PsI) end. But processing speed of the mechanism is what we're witnessing.

Over the last 30 years, the body of knowledge of NLP has evolved at more and more levels of detail at lower levels of thinking. Consider the variety that we've created at both the Environment and Behavior levels (logical levels) by changing the content on various patterns. How many varieties of the same intervention do we now have? For example, when doing a parts integration, although the process is basically the same, we have infinite variety in the language we use and the layers of linguistic cues, visual images and sounds we use in what is intrinsically the same process. Not a bad thing....just variations along the same theme.

Given what we now know from the quantum revelations of the last 50 years, and were we to assume that NLP does indeed, track and label the functioning of the mechanism (somewhat like an owners manual for your car....), where can we now go if we are to continue to engage in our own evolution, building on what we already have and already know?

In a world that has taught us to defer to external references (i.e. parents, teachers, rules, laws, dogma, authorities, etc.), one of the first things we must learn is to ignore/distrust the internal cues that come from the body. NLP has made it possible for us to begin, once again, to trust the mechanism of the body. NLP has made the functions of the mechanism itself predictable; has made it possible for us to begin to trust that the body knows what it's doing with energy/information, just like we trust that the body knows how to digest our lunch. Consider that we might want to begin to recognize that if our bodies are bio-processors (and science, the god of the culture, tells us that they are), and if NLP does track and name the way the mechanism functions, if we were to step on to that platform and consider the view from there, we may begin to clear space for ourselves to get curious about: "What is the bio-processor, processing?"

A 'therapy' model would tell us that what we're processing is 'feelings' or 'emotions' – both of which are nominalizations. Today's science would tell us that what we're processing is 'information' – another nominalization and one that does not have attached to it the powder keg of consequences that go with 'emotions'. Were we to denominalize the experience, we would recognize that the mechanism of the physical body is a) engaging in b) moving information at phenomenal speeds. Dr. Candace Pert, in her book "Molecules of Emotion" would tell us that there are biochemical and electrochemical impulses that are engaging signals and transferring the information from that signal from one cell to the next, at speeds that defy our ability to comprehend (processing speed).

In today's world, as we begin to engage the world from a quantum biological perspective rather than just talk about it, NLP Practitioners hold the potential not just to learn the technique of NLP (i.e. read the owners manual) but to use the technique of NLP to bridge to trusting the natural intelligence of the mechanism of the body; be willing to allow the body to do what it's designed to do; get out of our own way, and allow for more information to move faster. ENGAGE life – to not only discover who we are but who we are capable of becoming!

In today's world, Practitioners hold the potential to have NLP be the invitation to their own discovery; slip into the background and open a gateway to the magic that unfolds when we can trust – 100% and without exception – the quantum biological mechanism that we are. Without NLP, our ability to trust is limited and prevents us from letting go and allowing our bodies to do what they know how to do… brilliantly, at break-neck speeds, without error and generatively.

We already know from science that every time we think a new thought, the topography of the brain is altered, allowing us to become a new perceptual filter for our own experience (or the creation of it?!). Imagine what life could become were we to allow these new thoughts to be engaged, from moment to moment, without fear.

In today's world, after years of experiencing and expressing NLP at the level of the mechanism, is it enough to continue to stay at that level of expression? Until now, the alternative has been to move to the content of the behavior and its results, with painstaking detail, (therapy model – slow processing speed). We have moved from that which is apparent – observable behaviors and language; to that which has been more subtle – the underlying mechanism that has allowed for these to manifest in space and time; to the next layer – the signals that the mechanism is engaging and which are resulting in these expressions.

Steps to engaging the Self

Step 1 – Breathe! As we breathe, the mechanism of the body opens and relaxes. In this state, the organic processor that we are expands and information/energy moves easily and freely through the 'system', in massive amounts. Details (pictures, sounds, etc.) are not always available and, given what we now know about the body, are completely unnecessary. However, trust is essential.

Step 2 – Follow the impulse! As the information/energy moves in the body, follow these sensations or impulses, to where they lead. Using the sense of safety that comes with the understanding that NLP allows for, we trust the mechanism of the body to do what it is designed to do and allow the impulses to be processed, without the need for content (i.e. pictures, sounds, etc). After all, we already know that there is no content in content worth knowing.[4]

Step 3 – Allow yourself to know the truth. As the impulses move, and as the bio-processor that you are 'metabolizes' the information that it carries, your body comes to a place, to a moment, of stillness. In that moment, the undeniable truth of your experience reveals itself to you. With this revelation, the topography of the brain is altered and your world is never the same again. (We instinctively know this, which is one of the reasons why we hold our breath and distract ourselves in ways

4 For details on the process of Quantum TLC™ and The CODE Model™, refer to "Phoenix Rising: The Freeing of Human Potential" and "Pathways to Personal Power" respectively, both by Louise LeBrun.

that allow the movement of information to be slowed or stopped completely. These distractions are often creative, colorful and tend to fall easily into the category of 'addictions'.)

Part III
NLP – Tomorrow

The Evolving Practitioner

If our bodies are indeed quantum biological devices that are organic processors, what are they processing? What is the 'information/energy' that is moving through these systems; and what purpose does this information serve? If NLP is the body of knowledge that will help us understand the body as a quantum biological processor, what do we need to be able to understand what is being processed? If NLP is the science of the processor, what is the science of the Signals?

Autopoiesis is the science of living systems. Simply put, an autopoietic perspective says that all living systems (and human beings are living systems) have an entelechy that unfolds. Living systems intuitively and instinctively know what is required for them to unfold; and these systems will engage the world with all forces available to ensure that this entelechy is expressed.

Think of the information that your body is processing as a dance of signals. We know, for sure, that there are at least three distinct signals that we've been able to identify. The one that we are most familiar with is the signal from our external environment. We'll call this Signal No. 2. This is the Signal that comes from our cultural conditioning; from the rules and regulations of who we should be. This Signal transmits culturally conditioned beliefs/values/attitudes that have shaped who we believe ourselves to have become, to date, and unquestioned and unchecked, will not only shape our future but the future of our children. This Signal comes from our parents, the church, our schooling and the cultural pressures we experience to 'perform'. Think of this as an external Signal, or external reference points.

The next signal we'll call the 'experiential learning' signal. This is the Signal that fires off when you're about to venture into something new, to try something you've not tried before, and says "Wait a minute! The last time you tried something new, you ended up feeling humiliated and went into hiding for weeks! Maybe you want to reconsider….". This is the internal signal that comes from somewhere inside you, usually in your own voice, that reminds you that the external signals are potent and have consequences. This bite has big teeth!

If there were only the external signal (Signal No. 2) there would be no need for the internal signal (Signal No. 3) because nothing would be challenged or queried. We would simply follow directions and consider the rules as real as breathing in and breathing out. But that's not how it works. No matter the strength of Signal No. 2, there is always a time in our lives when we begin to wonder… what else? What if……

That third signal, that signal that calls to us to press the edges, to ponder something other than the status quo, we'll call the signal from Self – or Signal No. 1. This is the Signal that we're born with; the one that is the small, still voice that speaks simply and quietly as we move through our lives. This is the voice that we call 'intuition' or sometimes, the one we think of as the voice of our god. Whatever we choose to call it, it is the Signal that distinguishes you from me; the Signal that moves us through our infancy and then, somewhere along the line, appears to become silent… or to leave us entirely.

As we gain trust in the mechanism's ability to do what it's designed to do, we become more able to get out of our own way! As we begin to reclaim the territory of the body, with a sense of comfort and ease, we become more willing to allow the body to process what it is best suited to processing the Signals! All of them! Instead of trying to 'figure it out' or 'analyze our way' out of difficult situations, we allow ourselves to relax into the information/energy as it moves and allow the body to engage and process the 'wave' of information. (What we call the 'deep structure of language' may well be the Signal from Self, with the integration/metabolism of the three Signals being the 'wave' that moves through the body. But that's another story.....)

As we engage these Signals – all of them! – we begin to notice that there is a complex dance occurring of the three signals inside us. We also begin to notice that these signals are moving inside everyone else we come in contact with. The dance of fractals leads to the dance of complexity as we begin to realize that every person we come in contact with has these three signals in movement, interacting with our three signals. If you consider what goes on in a family system, you can imagine the complexity of the dance!

What does all this have to do with NLP? If you are familiar with NLP; and if you've come to understand that NLP will make it possible for you to trust the mechanism that you are, you begin to notice that those who do not trust their own bio-processor must turn to the intellect (conscious mind, reason, analysis, logic) to attempt to manage all these signals. They attempt to use a mechanism that was designed to make sense of 7 (plus or minus 2) items, to attempt to manage these signals and the rate at which they move through the body.

We've been taught to distrust the body; to rely on reason and logic to understand our world. We've been taught that the body will betray us, will get in the way. And yet, in fact, it is our bodies that allow us to engage the world directly. The body engages life directly; everything else is a representation of that direct experience.

Staying in the tough conversations

With NLP as a foundation for understanding the mechanism of the body, we are now free to explore the depth of meaning of the Signals. We begin to notice that as we interact with others, our willingness to allow information to move easily and effortlessly through the body results in a level of awareness that is difficult to explain or replicate, without knowledge of the owners manual!

As we engage with others in this way, we begin to realize that there is pressure to go back to not noticing, to not engaging… to go back to sleep! Staying awake requires that we become willing to stay in the tough conversations and move through them directly.

As children, parents, spouses, teachers, medical specialists, etc, we begin to notice that our ability to stay in the tough conversations is directly related to our ability to allow 'information' to move easily, effortlessly and rapidly through the mechanism of our body. We begin to notice how quickly and easily we are willing to turn away from a conversation – turn away from engaging the world – when these Signals begin to dance and we are either unwilling or unable to allow it to flow. Rather than experience feeling 'overwhelmed', we shut down and reduce the volume and speed at which the information is moving. There are consequences for allowing the 'information' to be held hostage in the system of the body/QBP.

In NLP terms, we become more able to manage our internal states. The difference is that we are not attempting to eliminate them, or reshape them, or replace them with something else. We become able to expand and become more than, greater than, the experience of the state and allow it to be metabolized. In so doing, the topography of the brain shifts and we have become more.[5]

Signals Fading….

The greatest challenge we face is to be able to find and sustain Signal No. 1 – the signal from Self. Although we arrive with it and as such, know exactly what to do when we're tired, hungry or wet, over time the Signals of external environment and learned experience can begin to compete for our attention. Do we listen for that small, simple voice inside ourselves, or do we listen for the authority figures in our lives? Do we trust the truth of our own experience, particularly when that truth is in contravention of what others in positions of leverage might want us to sustain?

---

5 Refer to "Phoenix Rising: The Freeing of Human Potential" by Louise LeBrun for more on the process of Quantum TLC™

As our Signal from Self fades, so does our interest in life. By the time we arrive in our late 30's to mid 40's, we've already become jaded and distrustful of the promise of life. Having done it all – followed the rules and bought the package – we begin to wonder....is this all there is?

We become more able to listen for that Signal when we can trust the mechanism that processes it.....our body. With the knowledge of NLP, we learn to trust the strength and power of the mechanism itself and begin to redirect our attention to maker finer and finer distinctions in the Signals.

When Signal No. 1 - the Signal from Self - moves, we have learned how to listen.

The Evolving Master Practitioner: The contagion factor

The science of the mechanism is NLP. The science of the signals is found in a WEL-Systems approach to evolution.

In an NLP framework, distinctions in ability to perform are made by the way the information is taught and 'learned'. This learning is demonstrated by an ability to repeat and apply this knowledge as an end in itself. For example, the ability to effectively apply and/or demonstrate a 'phobia cure' (evidenced by the disappearance of the phobia) requires that a phobia be identified; and that the technique of the phobia cure be used to eliminate the phobia.

Distinctions between Practitioner and Master Practitioner rest in moving from the application of component parts (rep systems and sub-modalities) at the Practitioner level to formulae of component parts (i.e. rep systems and sub-modalities operating in a specific sequence to form strategies) and patterns at the Master Practitioner level . Trainers are those who can enter into individual or group processes and impart this knowledge in a way that can be replicated.

In a WEL-Systems framework, the distinctions rest with the ability to engage the Signals. At the first level – that of awakening – the component parts of NLP are used to gain trust in the processing ability of the mechanism. At the next level, that of staying awake in the presence of those who are as yet unawakened, progress is indicated by an ability to trust the mechanism, make distinctions in Signals (the three of our own and the three of another) and continue to engage from Signal No. 1 without capitulating. At the next level, that of being willing to stand alone, proficiency is demonstrated by both the willingness and the ability not only to recognize formulae but to also recognize the complexity of nested living systems or fractals (family/home, work, community, church, etc.) within which these formulae or strategies operate and the willingness and ability to stand outside the norm, and engage differently.

Those who teach within this framework are deemed effective not only by their ability to impart knowledge but by their ability to be living examples of what they teach. Those who teach are engaged in BEING the experience rather than DOING the work. As such, those they touch engage moment to moment with them, in their own evolution, at a pace and in a way that honors the expression of who they are.

For example, a WEL-Systems:NLP Master Practitioner engages all the material at the NLP Master Practitioner level and does so in a context much greater than the technique itself. Rather than explore strategies and their formation; or beyond eliciting, utilizing, changing and installing a more effective strategy, we would consider all of the above within the principles of quantum biology and an autopoietic expression. For example, individuals within family systems within community systems, etc. would be an example of Nested Living Systems™. Exploring strategies within this context invites exploration of how the natural intelligence of a particular strategy plays out at all levels of the system. We begin to notice the evidence of these strategies and the way in which these strategies contribute to the quality of our lives. The simple process of this examination has already begun to surface the intelligence behind the existing strategy and once metabolized by the mechanism of the body, a new and more effective strategy has begun to take shape. Processing speeds. No need for content.

As we engage the mechanism of the body to explore the Signals, we also become aware of the notion of fractals. The notion of 'everything is a microcosm of everything else' (in logical level terms, "as above, so below") begins to take on new meaning. We begin to notice the natural intelligence of fractals and how they play out behaviorally, not only in ourselves but in our larger behavioral systems of family, community, work, church, etc. Our ability to recognize patterns and become effective in creating change is both expanded and accelerated. Our ability to be IN a behavioral system and not be OF that system is enhanced.

Our greatest test is in our ability to stand alone. As WEL-Systems:NLP Master Practitioners, we become more willing and able to stand in the midst of others and be willing to think for ourselves; to forge new pathways; to hold our ground in a variety of situations. Our ability to listen for and engage Signal No. 1 is strong.

NLP – What's Possible

There are those who believe that NLP has exhausted its potential in its current paradigm. Its current paradigm, or context, is a therapy model or world view. The science that spawned this context is not only dated, it is in many ways inaccurate. To continue to rely on this approach just because it is familiar and it has become habit is to ensure that we will continue to be taken hostage by our own limitations.

NLP holds great promise for freeing us from the fear of our own bodies; for reclaiming our sense of peace and alignment with the body and giving the 'intellect' or 'rational thinking self' a break! Imagine what our lives could become if we were to raise the focus of our attention from the lower Logical Levels of thinking of Environment and Behavior (the mechanism and its predictable expressions) and were to move to engaging the dance of the signals (Spirituality, Identity and Choice). Given that we know that each level of thinking is contained in the level above it, the higher you go the more profound your result!

We say we want transformation... enlightenment... empowerment. And yet, we continue to seek the result of 'spiritual evolution' through the mechanism of the intellect. It will never happen... it is too small. We are reluctant to consider ways of being in this journey of discovery that are not familiar to us. This quest is reminiscent of the driver who lost his car keys in the parking lot but insisted on limiting his search to under the lamp post because that's where the light was. It may make the search easier, and it will not produce the desired result.

NLP has cast much light on who we are. Over the years, thousands upon thousands owe not only the quality of their lives but sometimes, their very lives to the knowledge that Grinder and Bandler packaged and made available to us all. But as we stand on the shoulders of these giants of personal evolution, we would do well do recognize that in all things, we must move on. We must stand on their very broad shoulders and move forward to build a world in which we can continue to unfold and evolve and become. As in any journey, that this may require we move beyond what we know is to be expected. That we may be required to leave some things behind is to be expected. That we can take what we know and use it to create something entirely different is, as in all things energetic, part of the magic!

Continuing to offer NLP in its existing context of a therapy model will produce results. And it will not only limit our evolution but will result in our creating more and more content at those lower levels of thinking. It is impossible for us to NOT create! We are creatures with great strength of intention and manifestation. If we do not lift up our heads and our hearts and go higher, bringing all that we've learned along with us, we will create finer and finer distinctions at lower levels of thinking. This is not bad... it simply will not take us where we say we want to go.

Consider the following:

NLP has made it safe for us to trust the power of **what** we are. Imagine if we could come to trust the full measure of **who** we are... the Signal that flows through us. The combination of NLP and the

WEL-Systems body of knowledge – in tandem – as a framework for change, allows for depth and speed of movement that defy logic. It is not that one must be chosen over the other. What is the dance without the song? What is the song without someone to move to its rhythms and flows?

One simple thought prevails :

"To change your life, you must first change the way you perceive your life."[6] In a world where perception creates 'reality', the process that allows perception to be examined and restructured is the process through which quality of life will be manifest. And is that not what it's all about?

Breath moves… eyes open… and the world is never the same again.

This article is available online at:
www.wel-systems.com/articles/NLPYesterdayToday.htm

6 Trick of the Light